creating modern furniture

Trends, Techniques, Appreciation

by DONA Z. MEILACH

Consultant: Lawrence B. Hunter
San Diego State University, California

CROWN PUBLISHERS, INC., NEW YORK

Dedicated to
LAWRENCE B. HUNTER
The Great Motivator

TT
195
M44
1975

Printed in the United States of America
Published simultaneously in Canada by
General Publishing Company Limited
Designed by Shari de Miskey

Library of Congress Cataloging in Publication Data

Meilach, Dona Z
  Creating modern furniture

  (Crown's arts and crafts series)
  Bibliography: p.
  Includes index.
  1. Furniture making—Amateurs' manuals. I. Title.
TT195.M44 1975   684.1   75-12759
ISBN 0-517-51609-8
ISBN 0-517-524619 pbk
Third Printing, December, 1976

acknowledgments

Creating Modern Furniture owes its being to the enthusiasm and willingness to share among the craftsmen who created the myriad exciting examples. Most of them work in quiet seclusion thinking that few people appreciate their efforts in this day of mass production and machine technology. The greatest joy in compiling the material was meeting the artists, listening to their ideas, photographing them at work, and displaying the results of their craft.

I am particularly grateful to Lawrence B. Hunter (also referred to in copy and photo credits as Larry Hunter) who encouraged me, actually prodded me, to undertake the project. As a furniture designer and teacher of furniture design at the San Diego State University, California, Larry sensed the need for a book which would explore the work of individuals who are not necessarily concerned with producing designs for industry. He photographed several woodworking procedures and finished examples. His studio and workshop at the San Diego State University provided a source for many of the tools, and Larry demonstrated their uses for my camera.

My sincerest thanks to Robert C. Whitley of Solebury, Bucks County, Pa., and his son, Robert C. Whitley, Jr., for the demonstrations and photographs that illustrate chair making in chapter 5 and for many other fine examples in the book.

It is impossible to list everyone in the acknowledgments but I must especially thank some of those who received us enthusiastically in their workshops and homes: Milon and Mabel Hutchinson, well-known wood artists of Capistrano Beach, Calif., who also insisted we visit Jocko Johnson whose designs they admired. Jocko's workshop was a veritable gold mine of improvised methods and exciting ideas.

John Snidecor, Frank Cummings, the staff and students at California State University, Long Beach, welcomed us warmly. John demonstrated his steam-bending

v

methods, and I was privileged to sit in on a lecture that Frank gave describing a tour he had made among African craftsmen.

I am grateful to William A. Keyser, School for American Craftsmen, Rochester Institute of Technology, New York, and to Stephen Hogbin, Sheridan College of Applied Arts and Technology, Toronto, Ontario, Canada, for permitting me to photograph their demonstrations at the World Crafts Council Conference, Toronto, 1974.

Robert Dice of San Diego, California, created a rocker for Larry Hunter to photograph so the entire series could be presented. Tom Tramel, California State University, Northridge, escorted us to the workshops of craftsmen and then provided beautiful photos of magnificent pieces that were not readily available for photographing while I was in the area.

I must thank Charles Hollis Jones, Los Angeles, California, for hosting my husband and me for two days during visits to plastic fabrication shops that create individually the myriad items he has designed. My gratitude, too, to William Fejer, Institute of Design, Illinois Institute of Technology, Chicago, Illinois, for his demonstration of plastic bending and shaping.

There were so many other people whom I met, whose work I admired and photographed throughout the country, that naming them all here would require too many pages that are better used for displaying their furniture.

Mention must be made of the grand cooperation given by museum and gallery directors that led me to photos of sculpturally oriented historical examples in their collections and to contemporary craftsmen whose furniture merited inclusion. Thanks, too, to the manufacturers: Knoll International, Inc., Turner Ltd., Herman Miller, Inc., Jack Lenor Larson, and others for their cooperation.

My thanks to my typist, Marilyn Regula, Morton Grove, Illinois, for her analysis of my rough drafts and to Ben Lavitt, Astra Photo Service, Inc., Chicago, for his beyond-the-call-of-duty attention to my photographic processing needs.

As always, I wish to thank my husband, Dr. Melvin Meilach, for his aid and encouragement throughout the long gathering, writing, and frustration periods required to bring a book to fruition.

Anyone who wishes to contact a specific artist-craftsman for a possible commission should write to the author, c/o Crown Publishers, 419 Park Avenue, South, New York, New York 10016.

Dona Z. Meilach

All photos not otherwise credited are by Dona and Mel Meilach.

contributors

Alvar Aalto
Mark Abrahamson
Federico Armijo
Sherry H. Ball
Joe Barano
John Bauer
Bill Bayer
Lilian A. Bell
Tom Bendon
Cindy Blake
Douglas Blimker
Michael Bock
Marcel Breuer
Jon Brooks
Dempsey Calhoun
Jeannie Campbell
Altina Carey
Wendell Castle
John Cederquist
Maximiliano F. Chavez
Frank E. Cummings III
Dan Dailey
James Danisch
Hal E. Davis
Roger Deatherage
De Pas
Piero de Rossi
Robert Dice
Pat Diska
Guido Drocco
D'Urbino
Charles Eames
Phyllis Epstein
Wharton Esherick
Bob Falwell
William Fejer
Ruth Francken
Antoni Gaudi
John Gaughan

Frank O. Gehry
Piero Gilardi
Carl Gromoll
Hector Guimard
Julian Harr
Joshua Hoffman
Stephen Hogbin
Jack Rogers Hopkins
Lawrence B. Hunter
Mabel 'Hutchinson
Milon Hutchinson
Jack Inhofe
Ritzi and Peter Jacobi
Edward Jajosky
C. R. Johnson
Jocko Johnson
Charles Hollis Jones
Frances F. Jones
John Kapel
Mary Keepax
William A. Keyser
Frederick Kiesler
Sterling King
Candace Knapp
Tom Lacagnina
Kenneth Langston
William G. Leete
Edward G. Livingston
Al Lockwood
Lomazzi
Gwynne Lott
Carla McCartin
Donald Lloyd McKinley
John Makepeace
Ann Malmlund
Ralph Massey
Franco Mello
Ludwig Mies van der Rohe

Norma Minkowitz
Dennis M. Morinaka
Olivier Mourgue
George Nakashima
James Nash
Gaylord Norcross
Robert J. Olsen
Jere Osgood
Pierre Paulin
Frank Plaminek
Libby Platus
Svetozar Radakovitch
Giuseppe Raimondi
T. H. Robsjohn-Gibbings
Eero Saarinen
Shirley Saito
Vladimir Selepouchin
Charles Semser
Joyce Shettle-Neuber
Thomas Simpson
Paul Sisko
Terry A. Smith
John Snidecor
Geraldine Ann Snyder
Joyce Stack
Ed Stiles
Pat Swenson
Clarence Teed
Studio Tetrach
Roger Thompson
Stephen Thurston
Tom Tramel
Bud Tullis
Connie von Hagen
Hans Wegner
Dan Wenger
Robert C. Whitley
Andrew Willner

contents

CHAIR-TABLE. Jack Rogers Hopkins. Laminated American
black walnut. *Courtesy, artist*

furniture: function and sculpture

The character of furniture reflects the personality and taste of the people who live with it; it depends upon their life-styles and the nature of their houses. Throughout the ages, as painting, sculpture, architecture, music, and dance have represented the thinking of the times, so has the furniture. For example, the severity of line in the art of the Renaissance also appeared in the furniture. The baroque is represented in heavy, ornately carved furniture designed to fit the decor of the rooms. With contemporary life-styles and art movements so varied, it is not surprising that many new ideas are evolving about the furniture we live with and use.

The scope of this book is to present the current activity of designers who create furniture as an artistic endeavor rather than for mass production and the marketplace. The majority of pieces were created by the artist for himself or for a specific client rather than with an eye to production. Because of the handmade sculptural basis of the items, industry is not able to reproduce them economically.

In past centuries, furniture certainly contained many sculptural members; legs were ornately carved, backs were carefully shaped, cabinet fronts were curved, and sculptural ornamentation was used to enliven the surface. But the concept of the entire piece of furniture as a sculptural form having an architectonic spatial relationship as well as a functional form is relatively new to the modern world.

A review of the history of art shows that specific artists and movements have influenced subsequent art forms. So far as sculpture and the resulting offshoot of today's sculptural furniture are concerned, the most significant impact was made by the simplification of form captured by the sculptors Arp, Brancusi, and Moore. Yet, even before that, there were whisperings that good designs could exist without the ornateness fostered by the French schools of design.

The art-craft movement of the 1850s spearheaded by William Morris was felt

THRONE OF TUTANKHAMEN. The throne and the carving of beaten gold with enamel over a wooden base, show the furniture in use about 1350 B.C. *Courtesy, Griffith Institute Ashmolean Museum, Oxford*

throughout Northern Europe and its effect appeared in architecture, fabrics, pottery, glassware, and furniture for the next fifty years. The greatest impetus to a simplified sculptural basis in all these disciplines was further nurtured by the Bauhaus school of design which flourished in Weimar, Germany, during the 1920s and early 1930s. Designers nurtured on Bauhaus philosophy have made a lasting contribution to our design culture, and our everyday lives are surrounded by their creations. Some of their names are practically household words: Ludwig Mies van der Rohe, an architect originally from Germany, is best known for the Barcelona chair he designed that would be compatible with his buildings; the chairs are found today in homes, showrooms, hotels, and so forth. Marcel Breuer of Hungary developed a simple graceful tubular steel chair and you will find copies in schools, restaurants, and public buildings. Finland's Eero Saarinen is best known for his "womb" chair that one can curl up in. Harry Bertoia of the United States completely revolutionized modern seating with his wire diamond design chair, and George Nakashima from the United States is respected for his organically conceived wood pieces.

The greatest benefactor of the emerging modern furniture design consciousness was German-born Hans Knoll, a member of a prominent furniture-making family. With his background in the production of furniture and a zeal for good design learned from his father, a pioneer maker of modern furniture in pre-Hitler Germany, young Knoll opened a small company in New York City in 1938—a company that today is international. Knoll was tragically killed in 1955 but his lasting contribution is credited with drastically changing the interiors of buildings in America and throughout the world.

Other artists working independently of an industrial aegis also influenced the designers in every aspect of furniture and interior design. In wood, the name of Wharton Esherick stands out. An intensely private man, he is better known among architects, designers, and furniture makers than by the general public. Esherick left a legacy of his work in a unique museum in Paoli, Pennsylvania.

Yet the concept of a sculptural-utilitarian approach to furniture is not as new as we may think. In any study of contemporary trends, it is helpful, even essential, to look back in time. Early man created furniture for his personal needs and, given the nature of human ideas, he soon embellished it. The embellishment depended largely upon the materials and tools available, how the furniture was to be used, and the desire for status, which was directly related to the amount of splendor and opulence added to the basic form. The decor symbolized man's spiritual beliefs, fears, and aspirations.

All civilizations have not developed specialized furniture forms. Ancient Africa (other than Egypt) developed no forms more complex than the stool and rudimentary chair. Furniture was unknown among the American cultures of pre-Columbian times, Micronesia and Melanesia, and aboriginal peoples such as the Eskimos. Among the ancient cultures that did create furniture, the trends and tendencies overlapped one another; one style did not end abruptly and another style begin; rather one style influenced and borrowed from another and blended into a continuous development. Though the scope of this book is to present contemporary furniture, a brief thread of furniture history and significant styles is offered. For a deeper study, one should consult the bibliography and a specialized art library for books available that delve into the styles and developments of each culture.

ANCIENT CIVILIZATIONS

There are few actual surviving examples of furniture from the early cultures of Egypt, Greece, and Rome because of the perishable nature of the woods, fabrics, fibers, and leathers from which furniture was made. We often know the styles of furniture that were used only through the study of fresco paintings, pottery, ivory carvings, stone carvings, funeral offerings, and, in later civilizations, from illuminated manuscripts.

Beds, stools, boxes, and throne chairs were the major furniture forms of ancient Egypt. The earliest surviving pieces from the Old Kingdom were uncovered in 1925 from the tomb of Queen Hetepheres, wife of the first king of the Fourth Dynasty of the Old Kingdom (2700–2200 B.C.). The best examples, however, were from the tomb of Pharaoh Tutankhamen, ruler of the Eighteenth Dynasty of the New Kingdom (c. 1575—1075 B.C.). The great wooden beds found in the tomb were assembled with bronze hooks and staples so they could be dismantled and readily moved from one place to another as the Pharaohs made tours of inspection throughout their lands. Their beds and thrones were transported with them, but other furniture was sparse because of the need of portability.

Early peoples used stone blocks for stools or simply squatted on the ground. In time, a wooden stool appeared. Eventually backs were added, but these were

Designs of early Egyptian furniture are known by the drawings that remain on a wall painting from a Theban tomb ca. 1500 B.C. The chair legs are shaped like animals'. *Courtesy, The Metropolitan Museum of Art, New York*

usually on throne chairs reserved for the use of personages of great importance. No examples of "everyday" furniture have survived; only pieces that were considered good enough to be entombed with their owners now exist.

The royal furniture styles of Egypt were architectural and animalistic. Early pieces had legs that ended in bulls' hooves; later the lion's foot was adopted. In both cases the foot always rested on a pad and was characterized by rigid frontality. Inlays, onlays, and painted decorations were common embellishments based on religious symbols. Wooden furniture was usually put together by dovetailing or with dowels, and the most common woods used were acacia, sycamore, fig, cedar, cyprus, yew, and ebony.

At about the same time that Egyptian civilization was emerging, Mesopotamian civilization was also in its formative stage. Between about 3500 and 3000 B.C. and for nearly 3,000 years, the two rival centers retained their distinct characteristics, even though they had contact with each other from their earliest beginning and their destinies were interwoven. The documentary evidence for Mesopotamian furniture forms is derived from relief carvings. It indicates that the forms were constructed in the same manner as Egyptian furniture except that parts were heavier, curves were less frequent, and joints were more abrupt. Ornament was richly applied using cast bronze and carved bone finials and studs, many of which can be seen in museums around the world. Paint and inlay were not used as much as in Egyptian decoration.

Mesopotamia originated three features that persisted in classical furniture in Greece and Italy and then were transplanted to Western civilization.

First: the decoration of furniture legs with sharply profiled metal rings, one above another, like many bracelets on an arm. It is believed that this is the origin of the turned wooden leg frequently found in later styles.

Second: the use of heavy fringes on furniture covers blending the design of the frame and cushion into a unified effect.

Third: a typical furniture grouping that survived into the Dark Ages of Europe: the couch on which the main personage or personages reclined for eating or conver-

Classical furniture design examples appear as designs on
Greek vases. Kylix, about 480 B.C., is attributed to the
Antiphon Painter. *Courtesy, The Metropolitan Museum of
Art, New York*

sation; a small table to hold refreshments, and the chair on which sat an entertainer
—wife, musician, or so forth—who catered to the desires of the reclining guest.

We know much more about Greek furniture than that of earlier cultures,
thanks to the existence of painted pottery, stone sculptures, and literary descriptions
which incorporated the furniture of the various periods. Prior to the fifth century B.C.
the Egyptian influence, particularly in such motifs as the palmette, anthemion, and
sphinx, is evident. The Greek couch, used for reclining by day and as a bed at night,
probably resembled the Egyptian bed in structure and style. Occasionally the legs
were animalistic, but usually they were turned on a lathe and ornamented with
moldings, or they were cut from a flat wood slab and sharply decorated with incised
designs, volutes, and other patterns in high relief.

From the seventh to the second century B.C. the Greeks developed a wide
variety of new furniture forms. The throne chair (*thronos*) generally had a high seat
and a back of varying height, with or without arms. The legs, joined with stretchers,
were sometimes rectangular—a Greek innovation—and often terminated in paws of
Egyptian inspiration.

One of the most graceful forms developed by the Greeks was a side chair,
called a klismos, which served as a model for the Directoire and Regency styles in
the late eighteenth and nineteenth centuries. It was the first form to have an upright
back and rear legs carved in a single, continuous curve from one piece of wood. It
had a solid, broad, concave splat and a flat crest rail at shoulder height.

Replicas of the klismos chairs were magnificently re-created, retaining the
vitality and beauty of the originals, by internationally known designer T. H. Robsjohn-
Gibbings. After absorbing the ornate and baroque styles of the Middle European
countries, he became fascinated by the simplicity and dignity of the chair he observed
on the ancient Greek painted vases, terra-cottas, sculpture reliefs, and bronze statu-
ettes. He designed twenty-two models that cover the full range of Greek furniture
from the sixth to the fourth century B.C. From about 1937 to the early 1960s, the
chairs were individually created and custom-made for clients. In 1961, Susan and
Eleftherios Saridis, who are deeply interested in Greek archeology and are the owners

STOOL. XVII–XVIII Dynasty. Drah Abu'l Negga, Thebes, Egypt. Wood. An early example of turned legs supporting a concave seat. *Courtesy, The Metropolitan Museum of Art, Fletcher Fund, 1930*

GREEK RED-FIGURED LEKYTHOS. Fifth century B.C. A curved leg klismos chair, a low stool with animallike legs, and a pedestal stool show variations in early classical furniture. *Fletcher Fund, 1930. Attributed to the Eretria Painter.*

SEPULCHRAL LEKYTHOS OF KALLIS-THENES: Attic, about 430–420 B.C. Marble vase illustrates a klismos chair with curved legs and a curved back that conforms to the body shape more than earlier chair examples, and illustrates a great mastery of woodworking. *Courtesy, The Metropolitan Museum of Art, Rogers Fund, 1947*

KLISMOS CHAIR. T. H. Robsjohn-Gibbings. A drawing of the original chair was found on a 5th century B.C. Greek vase in the Ashmolean Museum. This modern replica was designed in 1934 and is made of Greek walnut with the seat strapped in leather thongs. *Courtesy, Saridis S. A. of Athens*

FOLDING CAMP STOOL. Tomb of Tutankhamen, Thebes, Egypt. The folding stool remained a necessary item throughout history up to the Renaissance. A painted design on the legs and the abstract flower design on the seat are remarkably simple in their design concept. *Courtesy, Griffith Institute Ashmolean Museum, Oxford*

of one of the finest cabinetmaking plants in Europe, Saridis of Athens, worked with Mr. Robsjohn-Gibbings. They created and exhibited a stunning collection of Greek furniture that would have delighted any of the original ancient Egyptian furniture makers.

Other furniture pieces used by the Greeks of this period included a stool (*diphros*) with four turned legs that occasionally were joined by stretchers, a folding stool (*okladias*) with legs that terminated in animal feet, and a couch (*kline*) that consisted of a wooden frame with a top of interlaced cords.

The Greeks also introduced the use of a footrest as well as a headrest. The table forms of this period had three legs in contrast to Egyptian tables which commonly had four legs. Around the fourth century B.C. a tripod table appeared with a round or oblong top and animal form legs terminating with claws at the bottom.

Greek furniture, beautiful, practical, and impervious to time, outlived the bright world that nurtured it. As the Greeks conquered, colonized, and traded, they carried their furniture designs to distant lands touching the Black Sea, Asia Minor, Upper Egypt, North Africa, Spain, France, and Italy. In sites as disparate as Luxor, Egypt, and the Crimea in Russia, archeologists have found crumbling models of original Greek furniture.

When Rome conquered Greece in the second century B.C. many of the Greek forms were adopted, but embellished and elaborated upon. Principal furniture forms were couches, chairs with and without arms, stools, tables, chest, and boxes. There is excellent documentary evidence in mural paintings, relief carvings, and literature. Extant examples are particularly the bronze furniture recovered at Pompeii, and partially preserved wooden pieces from Herculaneum. Woods such as maple, willow, beech, citron, cedar, oak, and holly were used. Ebony was used as a veneer. Decoration consisted of painting, or inlays of exotic woods, tortoiseshell, ivory, and metals.

Along with styles showing carved animal legs and other derivations from the Greek, Pompeian wall paintings illustrate plain, undecorated wooden tables and benches used in kitchens and workshops, and cupboards with paneled doors. Clothes and money were stored in large wooden chests with paneled sides standing on square or claw feet. Jewelry and personal belongings were kept in caskets of wood or ivory, in small round or square boxes and even in baskets.

MARBLE FUNERAL COUCH. Greek. From Macedonia.
Courtesy, The Louvre, Paris

MEDIEVAL EUROPE

Following the collapse of the Roman Empire during the fourth and fifth centuries, it is believed that little furniture was made except for the most basic needs and in primitive clumsy forms. Of the few pieces there may have been, comparatively little furniture of the early medieval European period has survived and these date from before the end of the thirteenth century. There are some important exceptions and probably the best known is the so-called "Throne of Dagobert." Evidence supports the theory that in the twelfth century Abbot Suger of Cluny added a rigid back to a stool which was believed even then to be quite old, probably of the seventh century. It is likely that it had been the throne of an early Carolingian ruler because it closely resembles the chair in a contemporary illuminated manuscript in which Lothar I is sitting at his coronation in 843.

The faldstool seems to have been a dominant furniture piece in medieval times and appears frequently in carvings, manuscripts, and drawings. Faldstools were most frequently owned by monastic and cathedral clergy, whose way of life was sedentary so they needed such embellishments for comfort and they had the wealth to satisfy this need. Eventually faldstools were decorated so they could be distinguished from one another and indicate the rank of the user. The faldstool evolved from Egyptian and ancient Greek cultures where it served as the chair for kings and other potentates and was practical because of its portability.

GOTHIC STYLE

By the fourteenth and fifteenth centuries, the unsettled times, rife with constant invasions and movements, were past and urban centers emerged. These fostered a certain class of patrons who desired the amenities of a household, and new developments in furniture design and construction evolved which later were named the Gothic style. At first, portability remained an essential concern, and to this end lightweight small cupboards, boxes with compartments, and various sorts of desks appeared. A nobleman who owned more than one dwelling place did not have furniture for each; he had one set that he carried with him. Then, if his castle was pillaged in his absence, his loss would be minimal. Furniture was so scarce that it was common for a visitor to bring his own bed and other necessities with him. Folding chairs and stools, trestle tables with removable tops, and beds with collapsible frameworks were dominant. Oak was used mostly in the northern countries and walnut in France in addition to local regional woods. Many pieces of furniture were polychromed in blues, reds, yellows, and greens but few have survived. In succeeding ages bare wood was used and paint was stripped from the furniture.

The significant style called the "Savonarola" chair appeared in Italy by the end of the Middle Ages. Though its X design was based on the faldstool concept, the Savonarola style had great dignity and stability. Sometime it folded; yet it did not appear "fold-up." Actually it became the transitional chair design between the portability of the fold chair and the stability of rigid forms that followed.

About the same time caskets and boxes were beginning to lose their formerly portable character. There was an increase in luxury among the very wealthy so some pieces became extremely opulent. The lower social levels also desired comfort; the result was caskets and containers that became bulkier and simpler and were never designed to be carried around. Chests used in living areas also served as seats and were richly and intricately carved. Furniture was made for more public rooms and included banquet tables, a tall back chair for the master, and cupboards that were

CUPBOARD. English XV century, ca. 1475. Oak. Peg and
grooved construction with a pierced Gothic design. This
was probably used for food storage. *Courtesy, The Metropolitan Museum of Art, Rogers Fund, 1910*

built in. The frame and panel technique of construction had been forgotten during
the Dark Ages and rediscovered to become a major feature during the Gothic period.
Other constructional improvements of the time included the introduction of drawers
into cupboards and desks and the use of the neater, more efficient joints such as the
mitre and the mortise and tenon.

Other developments of the fifteenth century that later found their way throughout Europe were reading and writing furniture such as lecterns and desks. These
originated in the monasteries and cloisters; examples can be seen in paintings and
manuscripts.

THE RENAISSANCE BAROQUE-ROCOCO

As the arts of the late fifteenth and all of the sixteenth centuries flourished, so did furniture design in Europe: Italy, France, Spain, and the Low Countries. During the Renaissance and the centuries following, many styles appeared, side by side. New designs and the characteristics indigenous to the designs of one country overlapped those of another. Many of the forms were derived from early Egypt, Greece, and Rome so that a detailed history would be too complex to deal with in a short survey.

Briefly, the growth of a wealthy and powerful bourgeoisie stimulated the building of more opulent, substantial houses and palaces and a demand for good furniture. Italian Renaissance furniture exhibits a strong architectural basis. The purpose of the piece, as in early Roman furniture, was subordinated to its form, which developed with a tactful restraint and beautiful, simple carvings. Walnut was the preferred wood.

The cassone, or marriage coffer, was one of the more ornate forms of the time and such great emphasis was placed upon them that great artists felt no shame in lavishing their talents in decorating them. Eric Mercer notes that "many cassoni can be attributed, with varying degrees of confidence, to such highly esteemed artists as Botticelli, Pollaiuolo; Piero di Cosimo, Uccello and Donatello." Often these coffers were gilded and painted inside and out with biblical scenes. Sometimes stucco was added in the forms of scrolls, cupids, grotesque masks, and with massive feet shaped like lions or other animal claws and raised on low platforms.

Folding X chairs with seats and backs of wood or leather were called "Dante" chairs and often used with the newly designed writing desk that was massive, though simple, as writing became a more general activity.

As urban areas blossomed, along with wealth and luxury, the furniture, from about 1500 to 1540, became increasingly elaborate and costly. Motifs, such as those Raphael had derived from Roman sources, were freely used as decoration and in Venice particularly, more so than in Florence, the use of painted and gilded surfaces was lavish. The trend can be noted in the Venetian paintings of the period. By the late Renaissance, the revival of classical styles by architect Andrea Palladio went hand in hand with the carving and florid, sometimes excessive, ornaments on the chairs, chest, tables, and cupboards of the time. Thus, as architecture and art reflected the way of life, so did the furniture within the palaces, homes, churches, and other public places.

The threads and developments of furniture history throughout France in the seventeenth and eighteenth centuries are exciting and varied. French furniture was among the first to be influenced by the Italian Renaissance and undoubtedly remains the most popular of all national styles to this day. Almost all European furniture from the latter part of the seventeenth century onward drew some inspiration from Paris; before then a French style did not exist and most pieces were influenced by styles adapted from Italy, Spain, and the Netherlands.

A national French style probably originated in the work of Simon Vouet (1590–1649), a court painter to Louis XIII and the teacher of Charles Le Brun (1619–1690) who was responsible for the decoration of the Hall of Mirrors of the Palais de Versailles.

Centers of furniture making in France were established at Fontainebleau, Ile-de-France, and Burgundy, where designers and craftsmen emanating from different countries eventually developed a "French" style. It was remarkably graceful and delicate, enriched with inlays of small plaques of figured marble and semiprecious stones, of marquetry of ivory, mother-of-pearl, and different colored woods.

The cabinetmakers were outstanding and the work of André-Charles Boulle (1642–1732) was believed to be among the most skillful in Paris. He was recom-

THRONE OF DAGOBERT. VII and XII centuries. Bronze. This outstanding surviving piece of furniture has bronze arms and back, and was made in the XII century. The base and legs of gilt bronze date from about the VII century. It is believed that Abbot Suger added the rigid back to an ancient stool. *Courtesy, Bibiiothèque Nationale, Paris*

FOLDING CHAIR. Italian (Lombardy) XVI century, ca. 1500. 34 inches high, 30 inches wide, 20½ inches deep. Walnut inlaid with certosina work of ivory and silver. Furniture of this century was made for the church, royalty, and the wealthy. The Star of David design suggests it may have been used by a rabbi. *Courtesy, The Metropolitan Museum of Art, Gift of William H. Riggs, 1913*

mended as cabinetmaker to King Louis XIV in 1672, and he developed a style of marquetry derived from Renaissance models—a style which now bears his name. In addition to fine cabinetry, he featured beautiful inlaid tracery and decoration with brass and tortoiseshell. He also created pictorial inlays in wood veneers depicting landscapes, figures, and flowers. His sumptuous designs enjoyed such success that they were emulated throughout the eighteenth century and for a period during the reign of Napoleon III.

The Regency style followed Boulle and his school, and the period from about 1715 to 1723 showed a modification of the baroque and the emergence of rococo designs. The principal cabinetmaker of this period was Charles Cressent (1685–1768), cabinetmaker to the duc d'Orléans. Originally a sculptor and bronze worker, Cressent designed furniture made with various colored woods and elaborately mounted in gilt-bronze. His later pieces were decorated with floral marquetry instead of the rich, contrasting woods and finely chiseled metal mounts used in his early work. Furniture, beginning with Cressent, gradually assumed a very graceful aspect with more curves as opposed to the comparatively severe architectural forms of the Renaissance and the heaviness of the baroque.

An outside influence appeared during the early seventeenth century with imported items brought to Europe from the Far East. Lacquered furniture imported from India, China, and Japan whetted the appetites of the aristocracy, resulting in

12

ARMOIRE. Charles Cressent (1685–1768). Cressent was a student of Boulle. This is one of his early pieces in the rococo style using fine woods and decorations of chased brass. His later, more ornate pieces contributed to the evolution of the style of Louis XV. *Photos, Musée des Arts Décoratifs, Paris*

ARMOIRE. André-Charles Boulle (1642–1732). Boulle is known for the elegant mirrored walls, inlaid floors, and paneling at the Palace at Versailles. He also elaborated the art of marquetry and raised it to new heights. His distinctive technique of inlaying brass into wood or tortoiseshell has been named for him, sometimes misspelled as "Buhl" work. *Photo, Musée des Arts Décoratifs, Paris.*

widespread attempts to imitate the work. Most successful was a varnish first patented by the brothers Martin in 1730 which was used to lacquer commodes, boxes, and inkstands. Items often decorated with scenes supposedly in the Chinese manner were called *chinoiseries.* As early as 1708, the painter Jean-Antoine Watteau had decorated the Château de la Muette with such subjects.

New styles followed and generally were named after the reigning monarch. Louis XV furniture was made of exotic woods—kingwood, rosewood, and tulipwood. Accompanying the furniture were the brilliant and detailed tapestries of the Gobelins, Beauvais, and Aubusson factories. Fine upholstery materials were popular and cane seats and backs were frequently used. The most characteristic furniture during the reign of Louis XV was a commode with a bombé (bulging) front, a serpentine marble top and bombé sides. Following these was the evolution of styles including Louis XVI,

SAWBUCK TABLE. American (Pennsylvania) XVIII century (1700–1750). Walnut and oak. The top slides to expose a built-in drawer. *Courtesy, The Metropolitan Museum of Art, Gift of Mrs. Robert W. de Forest, 1933*

a neoclassical style that stemmed from the discoveries at the ancient Roman cities of Pompeii and Herculaneum. This new classical appearance quickly surfaced in ornamentation; the actual furniture contours were modified a little later. Straight lines began to supersede rococo curves; cabriole legs were replaced with fluted and tapered ones. Now decorative motifs included trophies of arms and musical instruments, swags, husks, medallions, and Greek and Roman figures.

The French Revolution ended the opulence of the royal court and the extravagances that went with it. The furniture style that spanned the period of the French Revolution and the rise of Napoleon is known as Directoire, a transitional style that represented a reaction to the elaborate court styles of the preceding century. The neoclassical form of the Louis XVI style continued but gradually became more severe, with Greek and Roman motifs more consciously imitated, and Egyptian motifs were introduced as a result of Napoleon's campaigns of 1798–99.

The Directoire period revived the Grecian klismos chair and a typical piece was the Récamier daybed, so named because of its appearance in Jacques-Louis David's "Portrait of Madame Récamier," 1800. The ends of the bed had two outscrolled sides, one higher than the other.

French furniture through the middle 1800s vacillated between revivals of the earlier styles with more vulgar imitations and/or modified imitations of Louis XIV styles, rococo and Renaissance. One exception was a French *regional,* or provincial, furniture, which had the appearance of solid and practical rustic farmhouse pieces.

ENGLAND

The English cabinetmaker emerged in the late sixteenth century during the reign of Elizabeth I (1558–1603) when prosperity and stability brought a significant

14

BENCH. 1855–56. American. Shaker. Enfield, New Hampshire. 33 inches high, 61 inches wide, 17 inches deep. Pine and maple. *All Photos: Courtesy, Philadelphia Museum of Art: Given by Mr. and Mrs. Julius Zieget*

ROCKING ARMCHAIR. Ca. 1850. American. Shaker. Canterbury, New Hampshire. 47 inches high, 23 inches wide, 22½ inches deep. Pine.

TRIPOD TABLE. 1850–1900. American, Shaker, Mt. Lebanon, New York. 25 inches high, 18 inch diameter. Cherry.

Furniture designs by Spain's Antoni Gaudí are individualized, imaginative, fantastic interpretations of Art Nouveau style. Two-seater from Casa Battlo, 1904–1906. *Courtesy, Glessner House, Chicago School of Architecture Foundation*

CHAIR FROM CASA CALVET. Antoni Gaudí, about 1905. *Courtesy, Glessner House, Chicago School of Architecture Foundation*

SIDE TABLE. Hector Guimard. 29¾ inches high, c. 1908. Pearwood. The French Art Nouveau exponent, a sculptor and architect, used stylized plant forms in the furniture he designed. *Courtesy, The Museum of Modern Art, New York. Gift of Mme Hector Guimard*

increase of interest in the decorative arts. By the 1700s new forms of furniture began to develop. Daybeds, upholstered armchairs, and various kinds of writing desks were created including the bureau with the enclosed desk and interior fittings of small drawers and pigeonholes. Toward the end of the seventeenth century, much of the English furniture was influenced by concurrent trends in France.

When the disastrous fire of 1666 destroyed most of London, there was an almost immediate transition to the new styles of architecture including re-creations of designs from Roman ruins. Ornate and delicately carved wood was favored for furniture; caning was common for chairs and daybeds; the "japanned" cabinet with glazed and lacquered doors was popular.

Grinling Gibbons, 1648–1721, a Dutch émigré, was the outstanding wood-carver of the period. He worked with the king and with the architect Sir Christopher Wren in rebuilding London. Gibbons's skill was unsurpassed in his attention to and execution of detail; some pieces are so intricately carved they can be mistaken for finely worked lace.

Walnut wood began to supplant previously used oak because its compact grain lent itself to finely detailed carving. However, since walnut was expensive and difficult to obtain in large, well-figured pieces, cabinetmakers adopted the technique of veneering. Marquetry was widely used in the succeeding styles of the Queen Anne period (1702–14) which marked the beginning of many changes in English furniture design. The cabriole leg, derived from the French, first appeared in a simple version with a plain, rounded, club foot or a hoof; and later with a ball and claw foot. The cabriole leg, when used for chairs, was often carved on the knee, usually with a scallop shell ornament derived from Holland. Chair backs became lower; the top rail had scrolls or fiddle shapes. Bureaus with drawers and a writing compartment below and shelves above enclosed by doors were notable developments.

Much English furniture of the seventeenth century became known as Chippendale. Actually very few pieces can be dated or credited to Thomas Chippendale; rather the name is a generic one for English furniture of the period because Chippendale published a book of designs in 1754 titled *The Gentleman and Cabinet Maker's Director* which collected and organized the designs that had preceded his own work.

AMERICAN COLONIES

As in all colonial settlements, the furniture of the American colonies reflected the style preferences of the group from which it splintered. Interestingly, because of the existence of new materials and the time lag for styles and tastes from the home country to reach the colonies, some highly individual furniture developed. English walnut furniture was now emulated in pine, maple, and other easily procurable woods that did not have the grain characteristics of walnut; so had to be modified. Dutch and Scandinavian settlers brought individual furniture forms and, these, coupled with the French influence appeared in the average colonial home. Later a colonial Chippendale, which has become a popular collector's item today, was in wide usage.

Perhaps, most germane to the discussion of furniture as sculpture was the highly individualized, almost monastic simplicity of the furniture created by special religious sects, notably that of the Shakers. Shaker furniture represents a perfected design and is a symbol of a pure culture coupled with certain standards of excellence imbued into the way of life and work of the people. Shaker furniture exhibits a natural frankness in its use of the materials and in the simple, direct, uncluttered turning and shaping of the members of a chair, a bench, or a table. In one easy glance, it strips away the flourishes and curves of the baroque and rococo.

BARCELONA CHAIR. Ludwig Mies van der Rohe. Germany, 1929. Polished stainless steel with leather upholstery, 30 inches high, 30 inches deep, 30 inches wide. The famous, still extremely popular, chair was created for Mies van der Rohe's German pavilion at the Barcelona Exposition of 1929. It cannot be mass-produced by machinery and remains an expensive handmade design. *Courtesy, Knoll International*

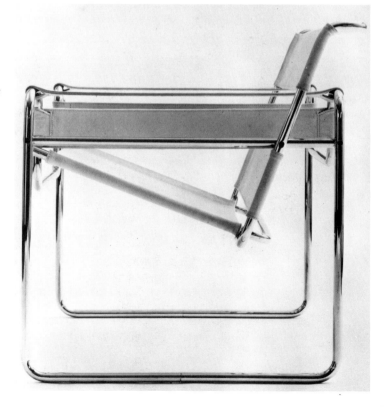

WASSILY LOUNGE CHAIR. Marcel Breuer. 1935. 22⅛ inches high, 58 inches wide, 24 inches deep. Polished tubular steel with canvas. The first bent continuous tubular steel furniture. *Courtesy, Knoll International*

LOUNGE CHAIR. Alvar Aalto, ca. 1934, 25½ inches high. Molded and bent birch plywood. *Collection, The Museum of Modern Art, New York, Gift of Edgar Kaufmann, Jr.*

NINETEENTH CENTURY TO CONTEMPORARY

As various earlier styles continued to flourish, the rise of industry brought about new developments which had a great impact on the production of furniture. During the first half of the nineteenth century, metal springs were introduced into furniture construction, making chairs and sofas much more comfortable. A technical improvement introduced into furniture design was the use of plywood which had great strength and stability and could be more intricately curved than a natural piece of wood. Another development was made by Michael Thonet (1796–1871), an Austrian craftsman who perfected a process for steaming and then bending layers of wood veneer and also solid beechwood into curvilinear shapes. His rocking chairs were popular during the latter half of the nineteenth century and continue to be made, not only in wood but in plastics and metals. His designs gave rise to the entire range of bentwood chairs popular in the early 1900s.

By the mid-1800s William Morris, often called the "father of the modern movement," was sickened by the shoddiness of machine-produced merchandise and opted for a "back to the craftsman" movement. He had many followers in the field of cabinetmaking including such designer-craftsmen as Ernest Gimos and the Barnsley family who produced small quantities of high-quality handmade furniture.

William Morris and his group gave impetus to the subsequent modern craft movements of the early 1900s. He influenced Henri van de Velde, born in Antwerp in 1863, to plant the seeds for the Art Nouveau style which flourished from about

CONOID CHAIR AND TABLE. George Nakashima. Chair: 35 inches high, 20 inches wide, 16 inches deep, American black walnut with hand shaved hickory spindles. Table: 77 inches wide, 42 inches deep. Single planks of English walnut with free edges and two rosewood butterflies. *Photo, G. Wm. Holland, Philadelphia*

1893 to 1910. The sinuous, undulating forms are characterized in the furniture and architecture of Antoni Gaudí of Spain, and Victor Horta of Belgium. The movement was also adopted in France where Hector Guimard was one of its chief exponents: his curvilinear metalwork can be readily seen in the grillwork and lamplights of the Paris Métro.

In the early 1900s furniture design in the West was either a revival of past styles or new designs that expressed the changes in modern life. The new designs were extremely fresh in their adaptation of materials and form. About 1925 the progressive experiments of the architects, painters, and sculptors nurtured on the theories of the Bauhaus in Germany, a revolutionary school of arts and crafts, often equipped students with the skills necessary to design for mass production. From this fountainhead emerged designers who greatly influenced modern interiors following World War I and continuing to the present.

Ludwig Mies van der Rohe designed sofas and the Barcelona chair to be compatible with the architecture he developed. He believed that perfection in detail and fine craftsmanship were essential to elegance. The timeless beauty of his furni-

ROCKER and SEATING UNIT or SCULPTURE PEDESTAL.
Frederick Kiesler. 1942. Rocker: 29¼ inches high. Seating unit pedestal: 33⅜ inches high. Both are made of wood
with leatherette lining. *Collection, The Museum of Modern
Art, New York, Edgar Kaufmann, Jr., Fund*

ture attests to his genius in proportioning structural and functional elements and to
his understanding of the nature of materials.

Marcel Breuer headed the cabinetmaking workshop for the Bauhaus from
1925 to 1928 but also experimented with metals and developed the first tubular
steel chair (the Wassily chair) and later the Laccio table/stool. Polished metal used
for mass production interested him and he was able to fashion the shiny surface into
an impeccable line in space so it achieved a visual and physical lightness. He considered his polished and curved lines symbolic of modern technology as well as technology itself. He thought of furniture as "drawings in space."

Other contributors to the arena of designers who explored the sculptural
quality of the industrial materials and the processes under which it could be made
included Florence Knoll Basset, who with her husband Hans Knoll, mentioned earlier,
fostered the creativity of the designers and the production of their pieces. Eero
Saarinen, Harry Bertoia, and Hans Wegner approached the design of furniture as
having to solve the same problems as the sculptor and the architect: space, form,
line, shape, mass, and volume plus a solution for function.

RADIO-PHONO SPEAKER. Wharton Esherick. 1956.
28 inches high. Walnut. Esherick's unusual application
of wood joinery and his individualized sculptural design established him as a master of a unique approach
to modern furniture making.

SOFA. Wharton Esherick. 1949–50. Chestnut wood
and upholstery. *Photos, courtesy Wharton Esherick
Museum, Paoli, Pa.*

The end of World War II saw the emergence of another approach to furniture
making by a handful of artists-craftsmen who were not so interested in production;
rather they worked individually creating custom-made pieces sensitively and lovingly
formed in private studios which may have been simply a workshop or a backyard.
Pennsylvania's Wharton Esherick's pieces in wood spoke well for the time and illustrated a mastery of techniques and new concepts which had far-reaching influence
among designers, furniture makers, sculptors, and architects.

Sam Maloof of California represents an emerging consciousness of the role of the individual furniture maker. Trained as an architectural draftsman, he made furniture for his home in his spare time. When someone saw it, he was asked to make a dining room set, and with that first commission Maloof became a furniture designer-craftsman—an almost essential combination. His designs are classically simple, meticulously created, joined and finished, with a result that has brought him a respected reputation.

George Nakashima, born in Spokane, Washington, in 1905, of Japanese descent, studied forestry and architecture. He traveled and worked extensively with architects, woodworkers, and carpenters in France, India, and Japan. Nakashima's emphasis was on the best use of a beautiful piece of wood in simple forms. He works "from the characteristics of the material and methods of construction outwards, to produce an integrated and honest object." Often his pieces contain the wood's burl, the crotch, or other unique natural formations and he uses them to advantage, rather than excising them or working with precut board lengths.

Another exponent of the characteristics of sculptural aspects of furniture design is Arthur Espenet Carpenter, who likes to think of himself as raising a prosaic utility, a chair, to the level of art, imbuing it with qualities beyond its matter-of-factness. "Espenet," as he is best known, specializes in one-of-a-kind wood pieces that have a direct appeal to the senses. Surfaces are smooth and rounded; they are comfortable and rely greatly on contrasting and richly grained woods that have eye appeal and the sensual characteristics of the natural graining and feeling of beautiful wood.

Wendell Castle learned from Wharton Esherick that the making of furniture could be a form of sculpture through appreciation of the inherent tree characteristic and its utilization in the entire sculptural design. Castle, an extremely energetic and sensitive person, has worked extensively with concepts of laminating woods to build up his forms. His concepts evolve from concern with support and are realized through three different approaches. The first is to treat the support, or base, sculpturally and as one with the sides and top, letting its form grow up and down and around like a living thing. The second is to have a small base, anchor it to the floor and—like a plant that will "come up with one very small stalk and still have lots of flowers" —have it support several functional units such as a chair, table, lamp, desk, etc. The third approach is to eliminate the base entirely and fasten to the wall or ceiling a sculptural support that flows into useful surfaces like tables and chairs.

Much of Castle's flowing, laminated works are blends of sculpture and furniture magnificently done. His style has had widespread influence upon the work of many of the craftsmen of the '70s. He is currently exploring similar concepts in plastics.

Several furniture makers are exploring the sculptural quality of furniture in materials other than wood. Craftsmen who have spoken against the plastic industrialization realize that it is here to stay and are discovering that the synthetic material can be bent to individualized creative ways. Pierre Paulin of France has worked with plastic foams covered with stretch fabrics to achieve a remarkably soft, pleasing series of shapes. John Makepeace of England, one of today's most versatile and sophisticated designers of custom furniture, works with any and every medium that will give him the desired result; wood, plastic, stuffed leathers and vinyls, furs, and others.

With these past influences as examples, today's designers, sculptors, and architects who turn their attention to furniture making, as well as those trained in furniture design, are continuing to explore the many new trends. The outlook is more exciting than ever.

ARMCHAIR. Eero Saarinen. 1956. 32 inches high, 23 inches wide, 23½ inches deep. Cast aluminum with fused plastic finish, molded plastic shell, seat cushion. As to the pedestal furniture line, Saarinen said ". . . the undercarriage of chairs and tables in a typical interior makes an ugly, confusing, unrestful world. I wanted to clear up the slum of legs. I wanted to make the chair all one thing again."

ROUND COFFEE TABLE. Eero Saarinen. 1956. 42-inch diameter. Cast metal with fused plastic finish. *Courtesy, Knoll International*

DIAMOND CHAIR. 1951. Polished steel wire.

SMALL DIAMOND CHAIR. Polished steel wire.

Harry Bertoia developed his wire chairs as an outgrowth of his interest in sculpture and his concern for space, form, and the characteristics of metal. He said: "In the chairs many functional problems have to be established first . . . but when you get right down to it, the chairs are studies in space, form and metal, too. . . . The chair has a lot of little diamond shapes in its wire cage, and they all add up to one very large diamond shape, and this is the shape of the whole chair. It is really an organic principle, like a cellular structure. *Courtesy, Knoll International*

SIDE CHAIR. Vinyl coated steel wire with elastic Naugahyde seat pad.

HIGH BACK CHAIR. 1952. Polished steel wire.

CLASSIC ARMCHAIR. Hans Wegner. 1949. 30 inches high, 24½ inches wide, 20½ inches deep. Solid teak with leather seat. *Courtesy, Knoll International*

PEACOCK LOUNGE CHAIR. Hans Wegner. 1947. 41 inches high, 30 inches wide, 29 inches deep. Ash and teak with a woven cord seat. *Courtesy, Knoll International*

Wegner holds his classic chair to be one of his most satisfactory designs because of its simplicity and harmony of parts in relation to the whole chair. There is a Grecian quality underlying some of the Wegner pieces and although his sophisticated handling of wood is frequently reminiscent of the finest 18th-century designs, at times his work has the forthrightness associated with Shaker furniture.

ADJUSTABLE LOUNGE CHAIR with OTTOMAN. Charles Eames. 1940s. A flexible unit that was designed for molded plywood and plastic furniture had a revolutionary impact on low-cost, popular design. The seat and spidery legs were imitated widely. *Courtesy, Herman Miller Furniture Co.*

RIBBON CHAIR. Pierre Paulin. © 1956. 29 inches high, 39 inches wide, 29 inches deep. Tubular steel frame covered with rubber webbing and preformed latex foam. The chair is beautifully articulated and the form is simple and direct with a solid colored fabric. *Courtesy, Turner, Ltd., New York*

The same ribbon chair assumes a different form flow upholstered with a fabric design by Jack Lenor Larsen. *Courtesy, Jack Lenor Larsen, Inc., New York*

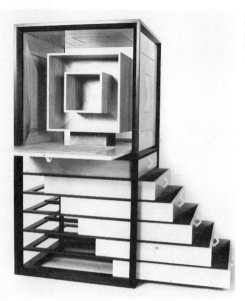

DOUBLE-SIDED DESK FOR A HUSBAND AND WIFE. John Makepeace. 1974. Macassar ebony, holly wood, buffalo suede, Lebanon cedar drawer linings and ivory handles. *© John Makepeace, F.S.I.A. Photo, Sam Sawdon, London*

MUSIC STAND and DICTIONARY STAND. Wendell Castle. Walnut. Heights vary according to individual need. *Courtesy, artist*

DINING TABLE. John Makepeace. Hardwood and cream lacquer. *© John Makepeace, F.S.I.A. Photo, Sam Sawdon, London*

LOUNGE CHAIR. Pierre Paulin. 1968. 24½ inches high. Stretch fabric over urethane steel frame. Mfg.: Artiford Co., The Netherlands. *Courtesy, The Museum of Modern Art, New York*

CHAISE. Olivier Mourgue. 1965. 25½ inches high, 66 inches long. Nylon stretch fabric over urethane steel frame. Mfr.: Airborne International, France. *Courtesy, The Museum of Modern Art, New York*

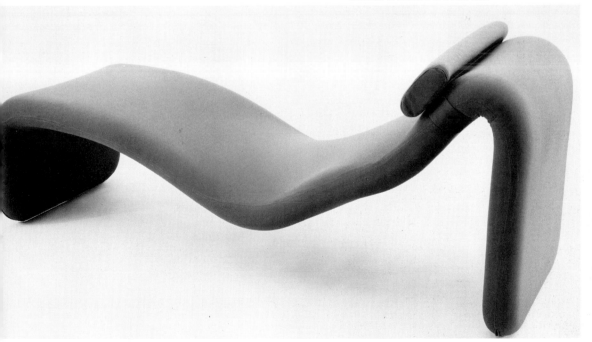

The craftsman's studio should be organized for efficiency and safety. California artist John Gaughan clamps wood shapes in a vise and then clamps the shapes together so he can work several pieces simultaneously with a rasp. Each tool's shape is outlined on the back board so it can be properly replaced and found again when needed.

2

basic tools, work area, safety

The contemporary craftsman takes the availability of many tools for granted. If he doesn't have access to a power tool, there are ample hand tools for the job he needs done; often he may use combinations of power and hand tools. It is hard to realize that the early furniture maker, home builder, and boat builder created very sophisticated structures using rudimentary tools. The Romans developed the first saw and also the first shears, the blades of which were operated by a flat spring. Iron was known by early peoples but steel wasn't discovered until the Middle Ages and then it was used chiefly for swords and other weapons. During the 1700s steel tools began to be produced. Finally, the development of tool steel, which is very hard and flexible, led to the manufacture of tools which were stronger, sharper, and more durable than any ever before known. Today the number of power tools is very great; but before the discovery of electricity, all furniture was made with hand tools.

Primitive peoples still use primitive tools and only a small assortment of them; consequently their production of furniture is sparse and often crude by modern standards.

The modern craftsman has a wealth of hand and power tools available to do practically every job from simple cutting to mechanical gluing. He can begin with a minimal number of tools, adding to them as he is able. Frequently, he can use the facilities of local industry, schools, and workshops. He can rent tools that he may not use often.

The dedicated furniture craftsman usually has a full complex of basic tools and these are shown on the following pages. Before purchasing power equipment, arrange for a shop demonstration or use the tool in someone else's workshop. Different manufacturers build in different features, sizes, and speeds. The beginner setting up shop on a budget might check ads in local newspapers for used machinery, or buy

31

outdated pieces from school manual training departments and factories that are dissolving their businesses.

Few artists feel they have the working space they would like, but all improvise and some astonishing works come from cramped, compact quarters. Larry Hunter advises the craftsman with a small work area to mount heavy tools on wheels so they are relatively portable. Improvisation in making a limited amount of space work well is the norm: only a few of the craftsmen interviewed have factory lofts and workshops with ample space. In warm climates, much of the work is accomplished out of doors.

Lighting for the working area is of prime importance; use daylight whenever possible, avoiding areas where dark shadows from window frames fall on the work surface. When using artificial light, strive for good overall lighting with extra lighting where cutting blades, drill bits, etc., are used; again avoid hard shadows from any of the tool parts.

When setting up a studio or work area, always allow for adequate ventilation and install a shop-vac to catch sawdust. Zealously observe the safety rules of woodworking.

The best tool to use for any job is the one that will best produce the results you want. This may be anything from a simple screwdriver to an all-purpose power woodworking tool with an assortment of attachments. The most commonly used,

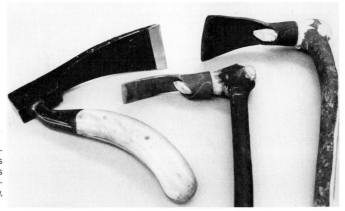

Hand tools have been used for wood carving for centuries by primitive peoples. Different shaped adzes are the primary tools used by African woodworkers to create an astonishing variety of sculpture and objects. *Collection, Frank E. Cummings III, Long Beach, Calif.*

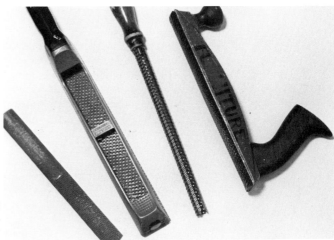

Wood files, rasps, and planes are available in several sizes. The common file shapes are flat, half-round, round, and triangular in lengths from 4 to 14 inches.

versatile tools are illustrated and discussed. Check catalogs from tool manufacturers for additional items. For complete instructions refer also to the Delta Rockwell Craft Library (*see* Bibliography).

There are basic workshop caution rules to bear in mind:

Always be familiar with the tool and what it can and cannot do. Practice on scrap lumber until you are familiar with its potentials and limitations.

Never allow yourself to become overconfident and try to push the use of the tool beyond its capacities. Do not wear clothes or articles that hang or dangle, such as scarves, loose sleeves, rings, wristwatches, or items that could get caught in the machinery or saw blade. Long hair should be kept tied back, safety goggles should be worn over eyeglasses as well as directly on the face. Always keep hands in sight and clear of moving blades. Never reach across a blade while it is running. Never try to stop a blade with your hand or pick a cutoff from the table while the blade is running.

Always switch the machine off and pull the plug out before you replace blades, drill bits, and so forth. Detach the power when you have finished working so that no one can turn a machine on accidentally.

Always think about what you are going to do before you do it and be sure every action you take is the safest; carelessness cannot be tolerated in a woodworking shop.

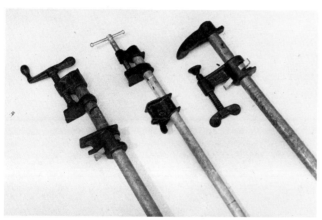

Gluing clamps, or bar clamps, consist of two parts placed on a length of threaded pipe. They can be opened very wide for large and wide processes.

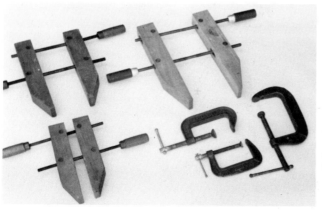

Several kinds of clamps used in furniture making will be observed throughout the book. Shown here are steel spindle hand-screw clamps with hardwood jaws, and C clamps.

Modern power tools are the backbone of the woodworkers productivity. They should be placed where there is ample light and working space for manipulating large pieces of wood. Shown are: *Left to right,* drill press, spindle shaper with bar clamps on shelf above, band saw, belt sander, jigsaw, wood lathe, and in the foreground, a table saw. *Photographed at California State University, Long Beach, Calif.*

Sawing and sanding wood, plastics, and other materials produce accumulated dust which is known to be detrimental to one's health. In Larry Hunter's workshop, the band saw and belt sander are vented so the dust empties into a shop vacuum.

In small workshops, tool portability is essential. Larry Hunter has a vise mounted on a heavy tree trunk placed on three wheels. One front swivel wheel and a handle permit easy maneuverability.

The table (or bench) saw is a versatile and essential power tool used for many procedures in addition to straight sawing. Mounting it on wheels gives it portability as well.

"Cross cutting," shown here, refers to cutting the wood across the grain. When wood is cut with the grain it is called "ripping." When cutting on the table saw always allow space between the board and the fence to prevent the board from landing between fence and blade after cutting is completed.

Assorted blades available for the table, or bench, saw permit the tool to be used for shaping, making dados, cutting plastics and other materials.

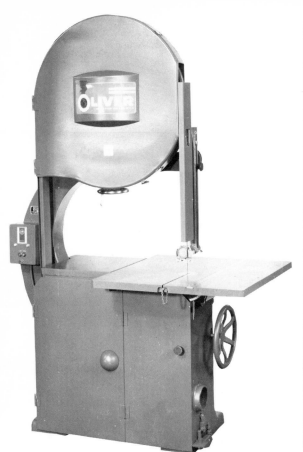

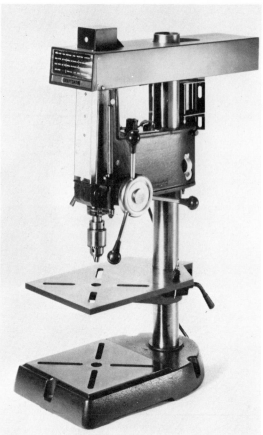

The band saw. *Courtesy, Oliver Machinery Co.*   Drill press. *Courtesy, Sears, Roebuck & Co.*

THE BAND SAW

The band saw is so called because the blade is a continuous flexible steel band with teeth that rotate between two larger rubber-rimmed wheels. The band saw leads power cutting tools with depth-of-cut capacity and cutting speed. It is efficient for straight line cutting when a fence is used. It is at its best for curves and irregular lines. The jigsaw (not shown) is used for internal cuts; its blade has an up-and-down motion as opposed to the circular continuously functioning blade of the band saw. The band saw can also be used for resawing.

THE DRILL PRESS

The drill press was originally conceived as a metal working machine, but accessories, modifications, and refinements make it a versatile power tool for wood work as well. The basic mechanism of a drill press is a power-driven steel rod, called a "spindle," with a holding device at the free end to grip cutting tools securely and rotate them. For wood, a press is needed that runs at very low speeds of less than 500 rpm. Large bits require even slower speed.

Wood cutting tools for the drill press are called bits and only a mark on the cutting work is required to start the point into the board. A block of wood under the work will prevent the underside from splintering and avoid drilling into the table and

The panel saw, most often found in commercial lumber companies, is beginning to find its way into private workshops and schools. It cuts large and small pieces of wood and plastic sheet straight and quickly. *Photographed at Loop Acrylics, Chicago, Ill.*

The radial arm saw does most of the same operations as the table saw but is superior for cut-off operations. The blade is brought down from the top of the unit; this differs from the table saw which has the blades protruding up from the flat surface. With accessories, the radial arm saw can also be used for drilling, routing, and other procedures.

A wide variety of power hand tools are available for almost every woodworking operation imaginable. A jig, or scroll, saw is useful for cutting intricate shapes.

ruining the bits. In addition to the usual metal and wood bits, assorted drills can be set into the chuck for specific operations. These include a spur drill, expansive drill, circle cutter and plug cutter, router bit, dovetail cutter, countersink, and a hollow chisel for mortising. Also refer to chapter 4 for use of specialized drills.

THE JOINTER

The jointer is a power-driven rotary cutting edge tool used for planing board faces and edges straight and smooth, cutting rabbets, chamfers, and bevels, planing tapers, and for specialty cuts. Jointers are made in 4-6-8-10-12-14- and 16-inch blade and table widths. The wider jointers usually have longer tables. The jointer's working principle consists of a round cutter head with 2, 3, or 4 knives revolving at a speed of approximately 4000 rpm in a small cutting arc that produces a series of tiny concave wedge cuts in the wood surface. Always use new and clean wood; check for sand or other hard materials which could chip the cutter blades. Used lumber may have hidden nails, paint, and other imperfections which could damage the cutter blades.

The wood is fed to the cutter head between a fence and guard. When the wood is too small to handle, use push sticks or support boards to hold the wood properly. Fences may be tilted to angles for cutting chamfers and bevels. They are also equipped with special adjustments for cutting rabbets used in joining.

THE LATHE

The lathe is a versatile tool for the woodworker who can use its power-turning principles for shaping symmetrical spindles, legs, and other parts. The spindle can also be offset in the lathe's holder so that asymmetrical turnings can be achieved. A round sanding drum can be placed on the spindle for sanding curved shapes. To operate the lathe, the wood is mounted on a face plate or between centers and is shaped by the use of hand-held chisels or special cutters held against the wood. The

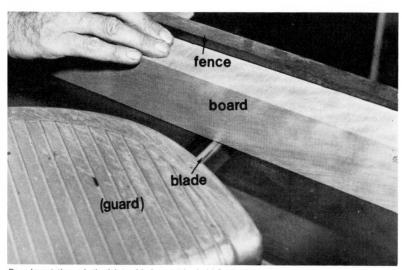

Boards put through the jointer blade must be held firmly with pressure on the table and against the fence to achieve a square edge. Feed the work through with an even steady speed; too fast causes ripples and uneven jointing; too slow may cause burning of the wood. The power-driven rotary cutting blade evens the board edge as it is fed over the blade and held against the fence. Keep hands away from the cutter head area. Plane with the grain to avoid chipping or tearing the wood fibers. When the jointer is running the guard should be in place.

angle, and pressure of the chisels or cutters, combined with the speed of the rotating stock determine the shape and depth of the cut. Hard and soft woods react differently and require experimentation. See page 168 for Stephen Hogbin's improvised lathe for making oversize turnings.

head spindle and plate end attachment

chisel

spindle

tool support base

spindle lock

The lathe is operated with a hand held cutting tool supported on a tool rest. The wood stock is mounted between two spindles and turned. For some shaping procedures, the wood is mounted only on one end using a face plate, and the cutting tool is pressed so it scrapes the wood to result in bowl shapes or routed details.

A range of large and small lathe tools, commercial and handmade. (You can alter tool shapes for specific cutting surfaces.) When sharpening these tools the burr is left on, to achieve cleaner cuts. At right, calipers, used for measuring are shown.

GRINDING, SANDING, AND ABRASIVE TOOLS

Grinding and sanding operations accomplish the final shaping of a part or bring a part to a correct size for final finishing. Modern abrasive tools have been developed for grinding and smoothing the most intricate shapes in odd places and at every conceivable angle or indentation. Abrasive tools used in the shop are grinders, disc sanders, stationary and portable belt sanders. These tools can do many jobs from rough sanding to precision grinding.

When choosing abrasives, there are three points to consider:

1.   Open or closed coating. On a "closed coat" the abrasive grains are closely spaced, presenting a full surface. An "open coat" has spaces between the grains so that particles removed by sanding do not fill or clog the surface of the paper. This is desirable when you are doing round sanding or removing an old finish.

New tools are constantly available to facilitate procedures. Assorted flexible grinding wheels that simultaneously sand and shape have wheels made of resilient abrasive cloth flaps. Various sizes, shapes, and grits are available for shaping, polishing, or grinding wood or metal. The wheels fit portable drills, bench motors, or high-speed miniature power wheels and flex shafts. *Photos, courtesy, Merit Products Co., Compton, Calif.*

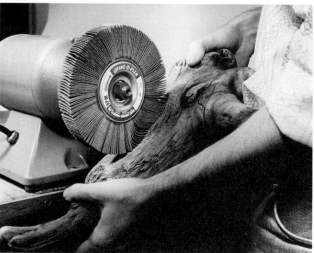

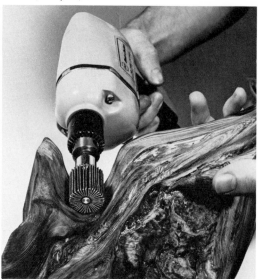

2. Correct abrasive. The minerals used in today's coated abrasives are an improvement over the crushed seashells once used. Those most often employed are: *aluminum oxide,* a manufactured abrasive good for wood and metal. It holds up well under power sanding and is used on hardwood, aluminum, copper, steel, ivory, and plastic. *Silicon carbide,* the hardest of all abrading materials, is good for sanding undercoats and for smoothing operations between coats. *Garnet* is generally used with power tools for abrading hardwood, softwood, composition board, plastic, and horn.

3. Correct grit. Various classifications of sandpaper can be broken down in terms of coarse, medium, and fine. Manufacturers have attempted to standardize the classifications and symbols used on abrasives (*see* Appendix).

Shown are different methods for sanding. (*Top*) A hand-held power sander uses a sanding belt. (*Center*) A sanding disk on a portable power tool. (*Bottom*) A floor model belt sander will accept a large board surface for flush sanding as well as small pieces.

The versatility of the router is convenient for the furniture maker; it is used to make inside cuts of varying depths, for decorative trim, grooves, and for some joinery and miterings.

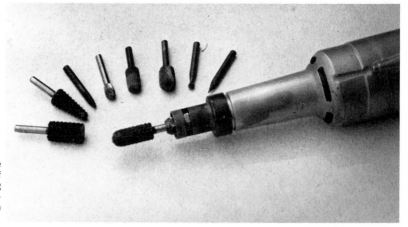

A portable electric hand grinder can be outfitted with interchangeable bits of different sizes and shapes for creating any number of specialized effects. Below, the bits and shapes made by them in a scrap piece of wood.

Two types of safety masks are available: Goggles (*left*) fit over the eyes and/or a pair of glasses and are held tightly to the head with an elastic band. The full face mask is hinged; in the down position it covers the entire face and it can be lifted when you are not working. *Courtesy, Merit Abrasive Products, Inc., Compton, Calif.*

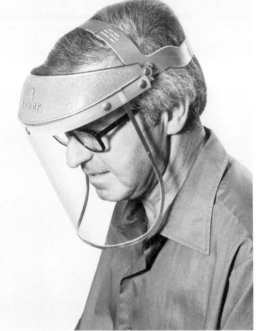

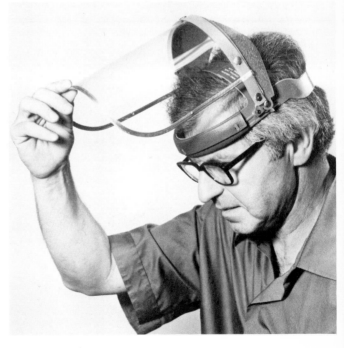

CHEST OF DRAWERS. Jere Osgood. Curly maple. *Photo,
George Landman*

3

trees, wood, logs, and lumber

THE NATURE OF WOOD

Wood has been used to make furniture more than any other material throughout history. Ancient cultures sometimes used stone; modern technology has added the range of plastics to furniture production. Yet wood remains the prevalent material for the craftsman working with sculptural furniture forms. Wood offers beauty, richness, variety, and warmth that appear to extend to and exude from furniture makers themselves.

All wood comes from trees, the largest plants grown by nature. Because nature is so variable, the wood derived from trees has so many variables that few precise statements can be attributed to the characteristics of the more than eight-hundred species. Certain general principles and approaches must be known about wood before selecting and working with it. Once you handle the material and are caught up in it as your medium, you will know that you must observe and be aware of its grain, density, growth patterns, and how it is affected by moisture and climatic conditions. You'll discover that the study of different kinds of woods and even the same woods from different forests throughout the world can be endless. To many craftsmen, this study is a continuing challenge. They attempt to discover new woods and how they can be worked into the designs they envision, to find the wood that will adapt best to their individual creations.

The craftsman seeking wood for furniture must be knowledgeable about his basic materials—especially wood, because of its varying growth patterns and its infinite vicissitudes. Knowing the essential tissues of a tree and their functions will help you recognize the woods that will best serve your creative purposes.

Trees form wood in the tall slender stems that support the foliage and bring sap to the leaves. Because of this life-sustaining function, every piece of wood is both firm and fibrous, solid to the touch, yet porous to air and liquids, strong but easily shaped.

The youngest tree shoots are green and soft; the first year of the tree's life they carry sap up from the roots and down from the leaves through the clusters of diminutive cells called *vascular bundles.* In the second year the growth begins, the scattered bundles around the edge of the one-year-old shoot unite into a cambial ring, or *cambium* which, in turn forms a sheath of very thin and active cells. This cambium layer lies below the bark of every living tree stem from top to bottom. It is so thin it can be seen only through a microscope, yet it produces, on its inward side, the entire wood substance of the tree's trunk and lesser stems.

On the outside of the cambium two thick vital tissues grow in every tree trunk. One is the *bast,* which carries a small downward flow of sugar-rich sap from the tree's leaves that feed the cambium and roots. The other is the *bark,* a protective layer that is created and renewed by its own thin *bark cambium.*

The bark protects the cambium and bast from harm. It resists attacks by squirrels and other forest animals, sharp frosts, and scorching sun. It helps to keep out fungi and insects. The inner bark layer starts out as *phloem,* a pipeline through which the food is passed to the rest of the tree. It lives a short time, then dies and turns to a corky layer that keeps moisture within.

Only in this environment, with these living cells, can wood be formed within the circumference of the cambium, bast, and protective bark. As the cells carry the components to the leaves that busily absorb carbon dioxide from the air, the magical growth process transposes all these elements into wood. This miraculous life process occurs in the spring and summer months during the active seasons of the tree's life and helps to create many of the differences in wood.

It is logical that the most rapid growth occurs in the spring of the year, caused by greater amounts of available food and moisture. This growth produces a wide, porous layer laid down by the cells which can be seen when the wood is cut; it is referred to as *spring* or *early growth* which is light in color, light in weight when seasoned, and moderately strong. As the season progresses, layers of darker, heavier, thicker walled cells develop and form *summer* or *late growth* which is very strong. When the tree is cut these layers that carry food up and down the trunk appear as circles, or *rings.*

Because these two layers of different types of wood are formed every year, they make up one *annual ring.* In many timbers, these can be seen with the naked eye and counted so you can judge the age of the tree before it was cut down. The oldest and smallest ring is always at the center, the youngest and largest on the outside. Though the rings are always formed the same way, they are often of different widths because of changing growth patterns that reflect the amount of sun and moisture available to the trunk in a particular growing season. The width of the annual ring is no use in identifying age, but it is of great importance to those who will prefer close-ringed or fine-grained timber for fine woodwork and prefer wide-ringed, or coarse-grained timber for structural jobs.

The annual rings of the tree and the cells that compose it have another characteristic. The *true wood* that is laid down within the cambium ring each year also consists of rays that radiate outward from the center of the trunk. The cells also carry food substances inward or outward through the trunk and serve as storage tissues for these foods.

When the tree is felled, and the timber begins to dry out, it shrinks along these annual rings; thus a log shrinks in circumference as it dries and expands as it absorbs moisture. This constant drying and absorbing of moisture is so great that it may force the wood apart and result in splits at right angles to the annual rings along the ray

The outer bark

The inner bark

The cambium cell layer

Sapwood

Heartwood

How a Tree Builds a Trunk

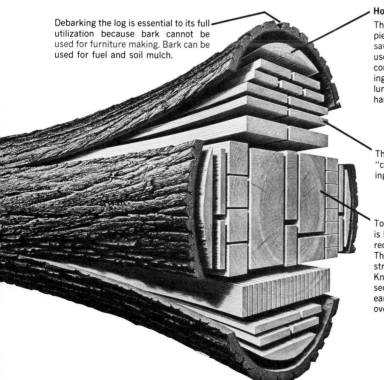

Debarking the log is essential to its full utilization because bark cannot be used for furniture making. Bark can be used for fuel and soil mulch.

How the log is used:

The rounded sides of the log, called "slabs," are the first pieces sent to the chopper as the log goes through the sawmill. This idealized picture shows the entire log being used for lumber, except for the slabs. Actually, as cutting continues, other pieces go to the chopper, including edgings, trim ends, and other parts of the log not usable as lumber. Each log presents different problems and may be handled differently.

The outer portions of the log have the fewest knots. This "clear" lumber is usually made into boards or planks varying in thickness from one to three inches.

Toward the center of the log, knots increase and the wood is less suitable for boards. Heavier planks, and square or rectangular beams are normally sawed from this section. The center of the log is used primarily for structural beams strong enough so that they are not weakened by knots. Knots are most frequent here because this is the oldest section of the tree. Branches that were removed during the early years of the tree's life left knots that were covered over as the tree grew outward. *Courtesy, St. Regis Paper*

formation. These are referred to as *medullary rays* and give the cut board some of its pattern. When drying is so rapid that the rays actually separate, the splits are referred to as *checks.* Other results of this shrinking and swelling movement are warping, case hardening, and honeycombing.

All wood is formed to carry sap. Therefore, it all begins life as *sapwood.* As a trunk or branch ages and thickens, the inner core is no longer needed for this purpose, though it is still essential for structural support. Slow chemical changes occur in the inner layers and produce a change called *heartwood,* essentially wood that has ceased to carry sap. It is usually harder than the sapwood that surrounds it and somewhat stronger.

Many trees, but not all, show a dramatic color difference between the sapwood and heartwood, and this difference aids in recognizing the tree. The difference in coloration and porosity between heartwood and sapwood results in unusual patterning sought by craftsmen.

Wood is not completely solid because of its cellular composition; each tiny hollow cell is separated from the next by a thin layer called *middle lamella.* The cellulose of the primary and secondary walls of each cell is composed of minute *microfibrils* formed into a threadlike rectangular cross section. The primary wall *fibrils* are arranged in a loose, feltlike mesh. The secondary wall consists of a fibril layer developed in a spiral fashion at different angles.

A short, thin-walled cell, the *parenchyma,* stores and distributes food. It is the living portion of hardwoods viewed with a high magnification glass. The ray is the longitudinal development of the parenchyma. The growth of the fibers, not the growth of the tree, determines the grain of the wood. The texture of the wood is determined by the size and quantity of the cells.

Another substance, called *lignin,* combines with the cellulose to form the woody cell walls and acts as a cementing material between the walls.

Wood is identified by such physical characteristics as cell structure and pattern, color, grain, figure, and sometimes by odor or taste. It cannot be identified by chemical analysis. Growth blemishes such as stains, sap streaks, knots, burls, cross grain, bird pecks, and shakes (a separation between spring and summer growth rings) and other markings may either improve the quality of the lumber or be considered defects, depending upon how they affect the strength and how the board will be used.

Wood does not decay naturally through aging, nor will it decay if it is kept constantly dry or always submerged in water. Conditions that affect the rate of decay in wood are moisture, temperature, and air supply. Damp wood can become an environment for wood ants, termites, and other insects.

SOFTWOOD AND HARDWOOD

Wood is named and classified as "hard" or "soft" according to the species of tree from which it is cut; the classification is botanical and does not actually indicate the degree of hardness of wood.

Hardwoods come from *broad-leaved,* or "deciduous," trees such as oak, mahogany, walnut, ebony, cherry, maple, and hickory. The hardwoods are strong and durable and more often adapted to furniture making than the soft woods. The reason is that they are close-grained with very fine, small pores. The close-grain woods inhibit splintering, chipping, and denting and are more desirable and durable than are the softwoods.

Softwoods come from *needle-bearing,* or "coniferous," trees including pine, fir, hemlock, holly, and all evergreens. Softwoods have large, open grains and are nonporous. The grain may or may not be conducive to natural finishing depending upon the quality of the wood. Softwoods are easy to carve, saw, and nail but they do tend to split and dent. The grains are not as beautiful as those of the hardwoods. When they are used for furniture construction, they are often painted rather than finished naturally. With the exception of redwood, most softwoods tend to deteriorate more readily than hardwoods.

SAWING CONSIDERATIONS: GRAIN AND FIGURE

When boards are cut vertically from a log, the grain pattern is evident. The grain, the result of the tree's growth, differs depending on the seasonal change in the tree. During greatest growth, the grain often becomes more pronounced, and sometimes very unusual, and this is referred to as the "figure." Both grain and figure are extremely important to the furniture designer who may want to match the patterns in two pieces of board when he designs a table or cabinet.

Figure can be matched by preplanning when sawing the wood from the log; this requires careful study and experience with trees, their growth designs and unusual features. Oak, walnut, zebrawood, and rosewood are highly figured woods because they experience a rapid summer growth period. Mahogany grows at a more uniform rate during the growing season so its pattern is more regular. Ebony usually has only grain and no figure. As the tree matures, the growth rings change; therefore pieces of wood cut from low, middle, or high portions of the same tree will differ greatly. If boards are cut straight (plain-sawed) or on an angle (quartersawed) the appearance of the figure will also be affected.

The furniture designer will purposely seek unusual figuring in logs and dressed board that appears in the crotches or V-like areas where the trunk separates into branches. Burls, which are domelike outgrowths from the trunk caused by broken or cut branches, are highly figured because the fibers expand, compress, and encircle the growth. Knots, caused by branches breaking, often are found within the tree's trunk between and within the rings.

The designer who gathers, cures, and saws his own tree trunks can take better advantage of nature's vicissitudes than those who purchase dressed boards. Robert C. Whitley's highly figured tables created from trees he has cut down, dried, stored, and sawed are prime examples (pages 112–115).

How a Tree Is Sawed.

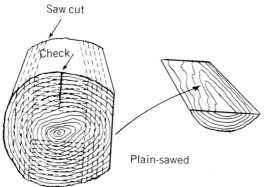

Plain-sawed

Plain sawed lumber has little waste, it is cheaper, easier to kiln dry, and yields wider boards than other methods of sawing. Boards tend to warp and figures may be strong and attractive.

In rift sawing, the log is trimmed to a square. Boards are cut on angles to the annual rings and narrow toward the center. A balanced grain pattern results.

Quartersawed wood is cut on an angle to the heartwood. It shrinks and checks and splits less than wood cut by other sawing methods. More figuring results; the wood is more expensive because there is more waste.

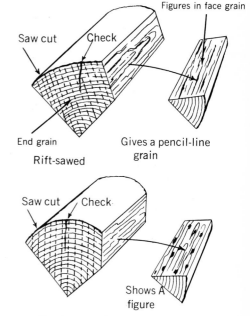

Rift-sawed

Gives a pencil-line grain

Quarter-sawed

Shows A figure

Lawrence B. Hunter (*left*) and Sterling King check their cache of walnut tree stumps dug from a farmer's property. The stumps are left to air dry for about two years in the southern California sun protected by a wooden sun screen.

SELECTING WOOD

Wood used by furniture designers may be from logs or dressed lumber. Much depends on the individual's preference, and, often, energy. Working directly with a log becomes a challenge for some craftsmen. Using the original organic form and developing it into a sculptural piece of furniture require excellent artistic vision and careful planning. The process is subtractive, and once the unwanted portions are cut away, the die is cast for the shape of the chair. Additional pieces can be laminated to the log, to expand it in various ways; portions of logs can be attached to one another by joining and laminating techniques.

Logs applicable to furniture are not always easy to secure; Larry Hunter and Sterling King go to great lengths to dig up black walnut stumps in Southern California. To gather this free raw material they place a hoist on an old mail truck to transport the logs and then find a place where they can be stored and cured.

Other craftsmen report that they find logs and stumps in forests and open land; they use ingenuity to secure stumps from farmers and from developers who clear land for housing. It's a matter of keeping your eyes open, having a truck available, and recognizing a piece of wood that is solid, not insect infested, and that may yield an exciting piece of furniture. Keep a tree identification booklet with you so you can identify a tree as one you want before you begin to dig.

The second source for wood is dressed lumber available from lumberyards in a variety of board sizes, lengths, widths, and grades. Certain companies specialize in rare, exotic woods for custom furniture designers; their ads may be found in art, furniture design, architecture, and woodworkers' publications. Write for catalogs or samples of wood.

Become familiar with the lumberman's terms by referring to any of the government publications or specialized books about lumber listed in the Appendix. You should become familiar with lumber grade and wood measures.

Dressed lumber, air dried and ready for marketing. *Courtesy, California Redwood Association, San Francisco, Calif.*

GRADING

After rough sawing, lumber is sorted into different grades established by the lumber industry. The two broad classifications are "select" and "common." Select is graded A to C. Common is graded Nos. 1 to 4. Prices are related to quality.

SELECT

A. Top quality usually sold for furniture by specialty wood companies. It is the most nearly perfect and blemish-free wood available.

B. Blemish-free: sometimes "B and better."

C. Small defects such as knots, slightly torn grain, highly variable coloring.

COMMON

1. Contains pieces with only small defects. Knots are always sound and fairly evenly distributed along a board.

2. The same type of defect as No. 1, but more of them. Most popular grade for all-around utility.

3. Numerous coarse knots or boards with loose knots and an occasional hole where a knot has fallen out. Boards are less uniform in appearance than 1 and 2. Includes boards that have been improperly sawed or that did not plane smooth on both sides.

4.   Rough, coarse knotty wood usually used for crating and certainly not for fine furniture.

Dressed boards are not the actual size that you ask for so always measure carefully; know board measurements and plan your projects to utilize available sizes. A 1" X 2" board, for example, is usually dressed to 3/4" X 1 1/2", a 2" X 4" is surfaced to 1 1/2" X 3 1/2".

Lumber is priced by the board foot, a standard measurement that refers to a board 1 inch thick, 12 inches wide and 12 inches long. Transportation is also figured into the cost of lumber. If you live near forests and mills, you will pay less for lumber than someone who lives farther away. Different trees are indigenous to specific forest areas so one should ferret out those native woods and use them whenever possible.

Used lumber may also be worked into furniture; such pieces can be found where old homes are torn down, or in old, quality furniture found in resale shops. Always be careful, though, not to saw up a priceless antique and make a coffee table from a rare commode, for instance.

VENEERS

In the seventeenth century, cabinetmakers who used scarce and valuable woods of beautiful figure and color soon sought ways to make the rare, expensive materials go further. Thus the practice of veneering became widespread; a plank of dark ebony or glowing, beautiful mahogany was sawed into thin slices and each slice glued neatly over the surface of a cheaper timber. Early cabinetmakers hand-sawed these thin veneers in straight cuts and discovered that a great deal of waste resulted. When the method was applied to a log on a true quarter it was possible to cut many more surfaces and reveal brighter grain than with straight cuts.

The next step was to employ a slicing process, rather than sawing, to eliminate loss of wood in sawdust and to hasten the job. These slices were then steamed and softened so they would be more pliable for use.

Today, several methods of cutting veneers are accomplished industrially, and the craftsman need only select the thin woods with the patterns he prefers and then apply them over a base wood by gluing and clamping.

When selecting the veneers of your choice, the stability of the wood is of prime importance so that it doesn't shrink away from the base wood. Veneers should be stored flat and in a dry place until they are to be used.

SEASONING OF LUMBER

When a tree is cut down, the cell cavity is filled with water; the moisture content may be well over 100 percent and the wood is termed "dead green." The evaporation of this moisture must be controlled if good lumber is to be obtained, as rapid drying

A book on trees and samples of various woods with the characteristics labeled on the back will help you identify logs and lumber. *Samples Courtesy, Frank Paxton Lumber Co., Chicago, Ill.*

BLANKET CHEST. William A. Keyser. 22 inches high, 42 inches wide, 18 inches deep. White oak, chestnut, and rosewood. Box joints used at the corners are structural and esthetic. The end grain of the joint is a texture contrast to the face grain of the box front. *Courtesy, artist*

Laminating and pegging are the joinery methods used in the detail of a table by Sterling King.

A dado joint with pegging is used to set a table leg into a tabletop. The pegs are a darker wood and this detail is repeated around the table. Milon Hutchinson.

A VARIETY OF WOOD JOINTS. *Drawings, courtesy, Popular Mechanics Magazine*

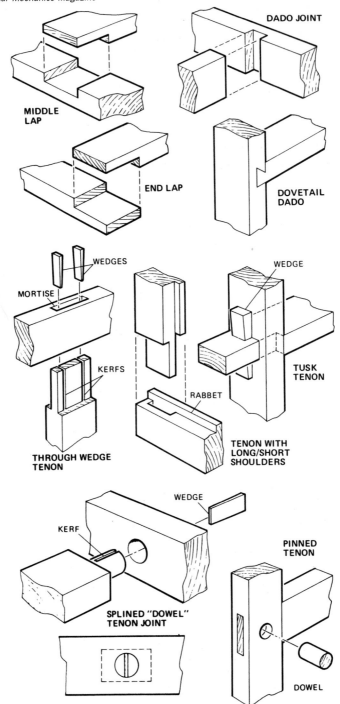

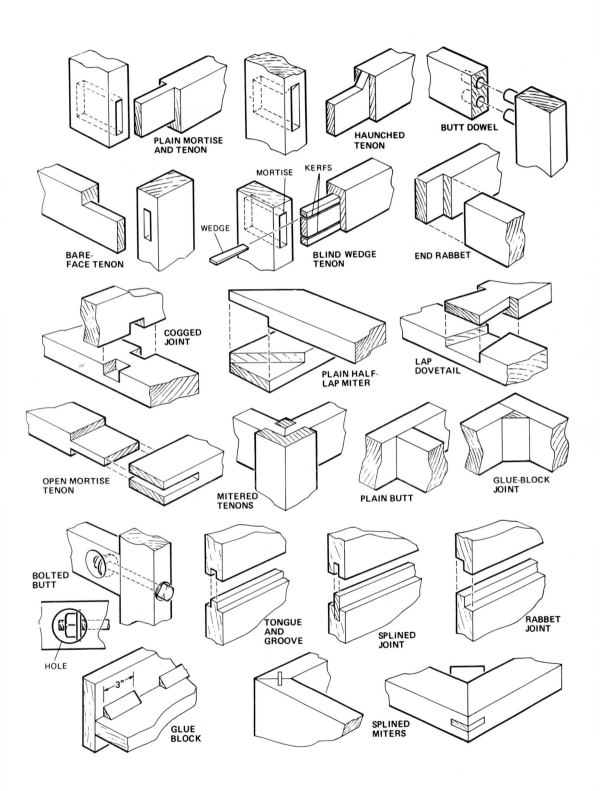

PLAIN MORTISE AND TENON

HAUNCHED TENON

BUTT DOWEL

BARE-FACE TENON

MORTISE

KERFS

WEDGE

BLIND WEDGE TENON

END RABBET

COGGED JOINT

PLAIN HALF-LAP MITER

LAP DOVETAIL

OPEN MORTISE TENON

MITERED TENONS

PLAIN BUTT

GLUE-BLOCK JOINT

BOLTED BUTT

HOLE

TONGUE AND GROOVE

SPLINED JOINT

RABBET JOINT

GLUE BLOCK

3"

SPLINED MITERS

The drawings on the previous page illustrate a variety of joints. The pictures below show close-ups of some of the joints in wood.

Butt blind dowel

Rabbets in different positions

Lapped joints

Dovetail

Box joint

Finger joint, a variation of the box joint

screws, pins, wedges, splints, dowels, corrugated fasteners, and other hardware. Glues are almost always used to reinforce the joint.

The strength of the joint depends largely on the accuracy of the fit to the joining members, the quality of the glue, and the efficiency with which the pieces have been glued and clamped. Other factors that affect the strength of the joint are the porosity of the woods being joined, how the glue adheres to the fibers and the degree of movement in the wood, that is: how much it swells and contracts under varying humidity conditions. The standard of workmanship is, of course, of utmost importance.

DOWELING

Doweling is a method for connecting and strengthening pieces of wood. Holes are drilled in each piece to be joined. The wood dowel, which is round with the grain running parallel to its length, is placed so that it bridges the two pieces. The dowels are glued for stationary joints. For joints that are to move, they can perform the function of an axle.

Dowels are available in 1/8-inch to 3-inch diameters, and in lengths from 18 inches to 4 feet. Better grades of dowels are made from hardwood such as birch or maple and are cut along the grain. They may be smoothed or grooved; those grooved with a spiral cut allow for a greater quantity of glue and a stronger joint. Ideally, the dowel length should be 2 1/2 times the diameter of the dowel.

Dowels may be completely hidden or they may be purposely exposed to create a design. When they are exposed, they must be integrated into the furniture structure and appearance. Sometimes, a false pegging can be added to carry out a repeat pattern of structural doweling. Doweling can be combined with other joinery methods such as rabbets, and a mortise and tenon.

A chair supporting wedge has dowels to strengthen it. Holes that receive the dowels are drilled the same diameter as the dowel. After the dowel is glued and hammered in, the remainder is cut off with a saw and smoothed, or it may be countersunk. Julian Harr.

Types of dowels: smooth, spiral cut, and fluted. Fluted dowels are designed to expand; they are made of lumber that is not thoroughly dried but which has been compressed. When used with hot or cold animal glue they expand and make a joint stronger.

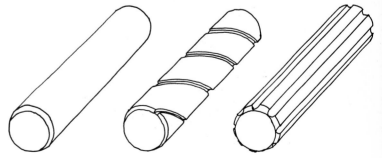

The dado is used for a variety of joining situations. It is a groove that is cut across the grain of a piece of wood into which another piece of wood is fitted. Dado joints are used in drawers, shelves, bookcases, table legs, and so forth. They can be made with handsaws or with the special dado cutting blades of a table or radial arm saw.

Blades for making a dado include two outside blades and a set of chipper blades; the blade (*right*) is a special circular wedge shape hub that lets you dial any width without removing the dado from your saw.

When using the dado chipper and outside blades, the wood should be fed into the blades very slowly to allow the cutters to work and to avoid splitting the wood at the end of the cut. Use a following board clamped to the work.

When the dado is to be made in the end grain, clamp another piece of wood to the piece to be cut and feed through the blades slowly and evenly. Also use the dado blades to make cuts for rabbet joints.

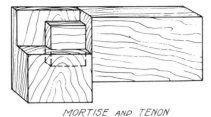

MORTISE AND TENON

The Mortise joint (made by a mortise and tenon) is one of the oldest joints used and is very strong; especially so for joining legs and aprons in table constructions. Basically, a finger, or tenon, is cut so one member is fitted into a socket, or mortise, of corresponding dimensions in the other member. There are many possible variations of this joint. It can be made with handsaws or machine tools. Generally, the mortise is cut first because it is easier to fit the tenon to the mortise than vice versa. To remove the waste stock around the mortise, drill holes to the measurements and then use a chisel to shape the pieces.

An open mortise and tenon joint is combined with a dowel.

Robert C. Whitley uses a mortise and tenon joint for the construction of a table.

PEGGING OR PLUGGING

The peg, or plug, is used to cover screw joints. A hole is bored in each of the pieces of wood to be joined; the screw is countersunk and a wood plug is inserted in the hole over the screw head. The peg, or plug, may be made of the same wood or of a contrasting wood for visual detail and design. The hole is made with a drill bit attached to the drill press; the plug is made with a special plug cutter.

Drill press bits and corresponding sized plug cutters. A circle cutter is at the right, bottom.

First a small hole is drilled.

Second, the plug cutter shapes a peg, or plug.

Third, the plug is fitted into the hole. In actual use, a screw is placed beneath the plug as shown in the photo following.

A rabbet joint is combined with plugging. A darker wood is used for the plug *(top)*. Below: a screw is placed in the plug hole; the dark plug will then be set over the screw.

A hole, ready to accept screw and plug *(left)*. At right, a plug has been placed in the hole and tamped down so it is flush with the surface.

A wedge peg is a strong and practical detail for furniture construction. The peg can be a dowel, or a round member turned on a lathe and shaped, as a round tenon. The tenon, or finger kerf, is split with a saw blade and a corresponding wedge shape is made.

When the kerf, or tenon, is placed in the hole, the wedge is forced in. The excess wood is sawed off and the remaining plug appears as shown at left. For greatest strength, the wedge must be placed so that it is perpendicular (at a right angle) to the grain of the base wood. If the wedge is placed parallel to the grain of the base wood, the base wood will split.

A circle cutter is a convenient attachment used with the drill press. It will cut diameters up to 8 inches and 1 inch deep.

The expansive bit or adjustable bit is used for drilling deep holes, as deep as any drill: The diameter of the circle is adjustable.

A pin hinge is often used in furniture design. The pins are dowels or rods and they allow a piece to pivot 180° and to both sides of the center. They eliminate the need for metal hinging hardware and can become part of the wood structure. The closing edge should be rounded for a tight fit. *All joinery examples prepared by Lawrence B. Hunter*

GAME TABLE. Lawrence B. Hunter. 26 inches high, 42-inch diameter. Laminated walnut.

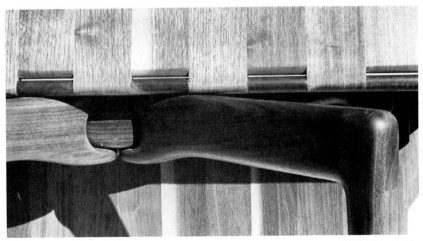

Detail of the pin hinge showing the tabletop and its underleg structure.

GLUING

Understanding glues and the proper clamping of glued joints is essential to the furniture maker. The success of the glue operation hinges on the following factors: (1) the adhesive selected, (2) the type of wood and its preparation; the joints must be clean and tight fitting, (3) glue preparation, (4) gluing and clamping operation, (5) post-treatment and exposure condition of the glued members, (6) joint or laminated design.

The following glue information has been compiled by Lawrence Hunter. Trade names vary and the same product may be packaged by different distributors. Generally, the adhesives are available in hardware stores and lumberyards.

LIQUID HIDE   Made from animal hides and bones
  Cost: Medium ca. $1.65 pt.
  Temperature: 70° or above, warm glue for cool temp.
  Application: Apply thin coat to both surfaces. Let get tacky before joining.
  Assembly time: Short, about 5–10 minutes
  Clamping time: 2 hrs. min. @ 70°; Sears = 12 hrs.
  Characteristics: First choice for furniture work and wherever a tough, lasting wood-to-wood
    bond is needed. A favorite for cabinetwork and general wood gluing. Because it is not
    waterproof, do not use it for outdoor furniture or for boat building. Very strong because it
    is rawhide-tough and does not become brittle. It is easy to use, light in color, resists heat
    and mold. It has good filling qualities, so gives strength even in poorly fitted joints.

WHITE GLUE   White liquid resin or polyvinyl. Made from chemicals
  Cost: Low, ca. $1.25 qt.
  Temperature: Any temp. above 60°, the warmer the better
  Preparation: Ready to use
  Application: Spread on both surfaces and clamp
  Assembly time: Very short, 5 min.
  Clamping time: 2 hrs. at ca. 70°
  Characteristics: A fine all-around household glue for mending and furniture making and
    repair. Excellent for model work, paper, leather, and small assemblies. Not sufficiently
    moisture-resistant for anything to be exposed to weather. Not so strong and lasting as
    Liquid Hide Glue for fine furniture work. Always ready to use at any temperature. Nonstain-
    ing, clean, and white. Quick-setting qualities recommend it for work where good clamping
    is not possible. High temperatures (100°+) tend to soften this adhesive. Excellent for dowel
    joint gluing since this adhesive does not become brittle.

CASEIN   Made from milk curd
  Cost: Low, $1.25 for 3 quarts when mixed
  Temperature: Any temperature above freezing; however, the warmer the better
  Preparation: Stir together equal parts by volume glue and water. Wait 10 minutes and stir
    again.
  Application: Apply thin coat to both surfaces. Use within 8 hours after mixing.
  Assembly time: Ca. 20 minutes
  Clamping time: 4–5 hrs. at 70°
  Characteristics: Will do most woodworking jobs and is especially desirable with oily woods:
    teak, lemon, yew. Not moisture resistant enough for outdoor furniture. Will stain acid woods
    such as redwood. Must be mixed for each use. Works in cool locations, fills poor joints well.
    Casein glues will bond wood through a wide range of moisture content from 2 to 20%. Two
    difficulties with casein glues are their abrasive effects on cutting tools and their wood-
    staining characteristics.

PLASTIC RESIN   Made from chemicals. "Weldwood"
  Cost: Medium $1.25 per quart mixed (comes in powder)
  Temperature: Must be 70° or warmer. Will set faster at 90°
  Preparation: Mix 2 parts powder with 1/2 to 1 part water
  Application: Apply thin coat to both surfaces. Use within 4 hours after mixing
  Assembly time: Ca. 20 minutes
  Clamping time: 16 hours at 70°
  Characteristics: Use it for woodworking and general gluing where considerable moisture resistance is wanted. Do not use with oily woods, such as teak or with joints that are not closely fitted and tightly clamped. Must be mixed for each use. Very strong, although brittle if joint fits poorly. Light-colored, almost waterproof. Mixing of the adhesive is somewhat difficult. Clean-up requires soap and warm water. Shelf life of the powder is good unless it becomes damp.

RESORCINOL   Made from chemicals—"Bordens," U.S. Plywood
  Cost: High; ca. $2.00 pint
  Temperature: Must be 70° or warmer, will set faster at 90°
  Preparation: Mix 3 parts powder to 4 parts liquid catalyst.
  Application: Apply thin coat to both surfaces.
  Assembly time: 30 minutes to 1 hour
  Clamping time: 16 hours
  Characteristics: This is the glue for any work that may be exposed to soaking: outdoor furniture, boats, etc. Not good for work that must be done at temperatures below 70°. Because of dark color and mixing, not often used unless waterproof quality is needed. Very strong, as well as waterproof. It works better with poor joints than many glues do. Resorcinol creates a dark glue line.

EPOXY   Made from chemicals
  Cost: Very high
  Temperature: Any temperature
  Preparation: Resin and hardener, mix in amounts stated on container.
  Application: Apply to both surfaces to be glued.
  Assembly time: Time varies, 1/2 to 1 hour.
  Clamping time: Clamping is not necessary, sets faster with heat. Time ca. 24 hours.
  Characteristics: Will bond wood to metal or other dissimilar materials. Use in combination with wood, tile, metal, glass, etc. Will not shrink or swell during hardening. Waterproof, oilproof, and nonflammable. Not good for fastening wood in large products. Must be used in well-ventilated room. Avoid getting into eyes. Can be painted, sanded, filled, drilled, or machined. Can fill large holes. Excellent for poorly fitted joints. Do not use on flexible materials or where stress can peel it from the surface.

UREA-FORMALDEHYDE RESIN   Made from chemicals, Urac 185; Plyamine 21–018, Reichold Chemical Co.
  Cost: High, $1.00 pint, less per quart and gallon
  Storage Life: 6 months @ 70° or below. Good as long as the liquid is pourable.
  Preparation: 3 parts liquid to 1 part hardener

Temperature:	60°	70°	80°	90°	100°	degrees
Assembly:	40	30	20	10	5–10	minutes
Clamping:	24	12	6	3	1 1/2	hours

  Characteristics: Highly water resistant, flexible, craze resistant. Excellent for furniture, plastic laminates, and veneers. Good gluing characteristics where glue line thickness and clamping pressure may vary. Glue line thickness to .020" is possible. Maximum strength is reached after 5 days @ 70° or above.

WOOD WELDING

Wood welding, called "dielectric heating," is based on the fact that disturbed molecules cause friction and create heat. The disturbed balance is caused by a very high frequency cycle change which moves the molecule of glue at such a high speed that the friction generates heat and the glue bond is completed in a matter of seconds.

The synthetic resorcinol and phenol-formaldehyde resins are easily cured with dielectric heating and are relatively immune to weather conditions. Urea-formaldehyde glues are less expensive than resorcinols but have the same qualities. Joints formed with urea resins are very resistant to heat and moisture. The strength of joints made with both types of glues increases with time.

Dielectric gluing is accomplished with a wood-welding unit shown opposite.

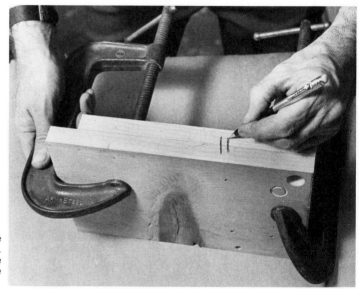

Always clamp the woods to be glued when they are dry and mark them for placement to one another. Once the boards are glued it is messy to unglue and sometimes the board will break before the glue line separates.

A urea-formaldehyde resin glue is mixed.

Use a brush with even bristles for spreading the glue; when bristle ends become worn or jagged, cut them off with a knife to obtain a smooth edge. Glue may be applied with a roller also, which is particularly good for large surfaces.

Brush the glue on the board evenly and amply; boards on both surfaces should be flat; any warped surfaces will yield pockets of space that may cause the surfaces to separate eventually. Recheck the registration marks and reclamp until the glue oozes. If the glue does not ooze, your boards are not clamped tightly enough.

Place the glue gun over the glue line for a minute or so. Shown, at rear, is the complete wood welding unit; the gun heating portion is connected.

Close-up showing the machine on the set glue line between the boards. The boards may still be pulled apart while the glue is damp. When dry, hardwoods will break on the glue line. With softwoods, the board will tend to splinter. *Demonstration: Lawrence B. Hunter*

VENEERING

Veneering offers the opportunity to cover a surface with rare woods or wood of special grain. The process consists of applying very thin sheets of wood (1/28" to 1/20" in thickness) to a core for the purpose of obtaining greater strength and a more attractive surface.

Veneers are usually strips or sheets of wood that are very flexible. They are purposely produced to take advantage of attractive grains, figures, and colors in rare woods. (Refer to William Keyser's table (page 166) in which a veneer of zebrawood has been applied to a core of plywood.)

Veneer sheets are sold by the square foot. They should be stored flat. The veneer is adhered to the core wood by gluing in the same manner as laminating. When clamping, a full-size board should be placed over the veneer surface and under the clamps to assure even surface adherence.

WOOD FINISHING

The cellular structure of wood requires the application of stains, fillers, varnishes, lacquers, paints, enamels, oils, or waxes to enhance the surface visually and totally and to protect the surface from dust and deterioration. Transparent and opaque finishes are applied by brushing, spraying, wiping, dipping, rolling, and rubbing. Finishes retard the absorption of moisture, fumes, and oils which cause the wood to shrink, swell, check, warp, and discolor.

Each furniture maker seems to develop his own formula for finishing woods. The majority prefer natural oil finishes that bring out the natural grains and colors of fine woods. These vary from any proportion either side of fifty-fifty raw or boiled linseed oil and turpentine to 100% linseed oil. Oil stains may be slightly pigmented or transparent. They are easily applied by brushing or wiping on. They preserve the wood and bring out the beauty without raising the grain and they produce a uniform tone or color.

Varnish stains seal the wood and may produce various tonal changes without altering the grain. Dark stains, for example, can be applied to pine or plywood to darken the wood according to the craftsman's esthetic judgment. Frequently, the stains are mixed and when the woods are treated with them the result is a subtle alteration that enhances the original wood.

Aerosol foam and liquid stains offer great flexibility of application. Always stain raw wood; then seal it with varnish, shellac, acrylic sprays, or epoxy finishes. Apply wax over the stained and varnished surface for additional preservation. Stains may also be made by thinning artists' oil paint with turpentine until they are fluid enough to be brushed or rubbed into the wood's surface and so penetrate the pores.

Coloring can be accomplished with any colorants available for wood such as enamels, paints, and acrylics. The wood must be sealed before applying the colorant. Carefully select the finish that will best serve your need; there are oil and water base, matte and gloss finishes. The type you select will depend on the purpose of the finished item. Consider exposure to weather and humidity.

After applying the finish, a final rubbing with a fine pumice powder such as rottenstone mixed with linseed oil will reduce any fine paint bubbles or imperfections. Waxing with a good quality furniture wax is optional.

PREPARING THE WOOD FOR FINISHING

Before applying finishes, carefully check all surfaces for dents, bumps, or stains. Remove any pencil marks by bleaching, if necessary, with a prepared wood bleach available in hardware stores. Leave on only long enough to remove the stain and not to allow the treated portion to become lighter than the rest of the surface.

Dents can be raised by using an iron and moist cloth, as shown. Or apply a drop of water to the dent and place a small cotton pad or absorbent paper soaked in warm water on the dent and allow it to remain until the grain is raised. You can also touch the moist warm pad with a hot soldering iron which changes the water to steam and causes the wood to swell.

Pores and other larger surface indentations may be filled with an oil base paste wood filler available in cans from your paint dealer. Color can be added for various shades. It is easy to rub off before hardening and it may be sanded after hardening. Synthetic resin base fillers are quick drying but hard to rub off the surface.

HARDWARE AND UPHOLSTERY

Decorative and functional hardware such as hinges, brackets, handles, and so forth are so plentiful in every woodworking supply source, hardware store, and housewares department that their use must be based on the preference of the designer. Unusual fittings may be discovered in catalogs from the many hardware design companies throughout the country. Sometimes, the woodworker will wish to design the hinges, hasps, and other hardware, and this may be done by forging, sand casting, etc. These may be made by a metalworker who can cooperate on the project.

Generally, the furniture designer should constantly seek the kinds of hardware that will accomplish the job; often he will discover unusual fittings such as the Soss hinge, touch latches, blind hinges, and magnetic fittings, and, knowing they exist, he can design the furniture accordingly.

Upholstery used in conjunction with wood furniture may consist of padded parts permanently affixed to the wood by nailing, or of removable cushions.

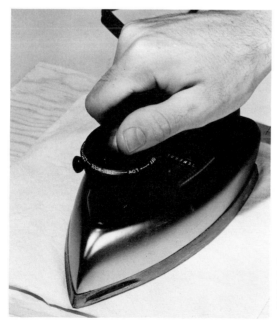

Dents in a piece of wood can be raised by placing a moist cloth over the bare wood and applying a hot iron over the cloth. You may have to repeat this two or three times.

Various types of joints applied to furniture: Two pieces of wood are joined with a rectangular "peg" *(detail)*. John Snidecor.

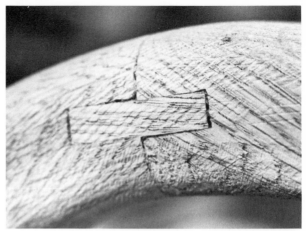

Removable peg with mortise and tenon and rope lashing *(detail)*. Jack Inhofe.

Dovetail and pegging *(detail)*. Bob Falwell.

A joint using multiple open mortises and tenons and various grain exposures *(detail)*. Bob Falwell.

Finishing a trestle table is accomplished by Robert C. Whitley. After hand sanding, a special blend of oils is applied with a brush . . .

. . . and then wiped to eliminate overlaps and to blend into the natural wood grain. *Photos, R. C. Whitley.*

John Bauer adds the final rubbing to a mansonia walnut conference table. *Courtesy, artist*

75

DESK. Robert C. Whitley. 44 inches wide, 74 inches long.
Made from matching slabs of a walnut tree. Compart-
mented drawers are mounted beneath the irregularly
shaped top. The smooth curvature of the base is a studied
counterpoint to the rough edge of the top. *Collection, Col.
James E. Bass, Washington, D.C. Photo, Jack Venettone*

5

creating wood furniture

There are different approaches to creating and constructing wood furniture. One approach is to begin with a large piece of wood, such as a log, and directly carve out the form. The other is to build up boards to the general size of the overall piece and then carve and shape the furniture to the design envisioned. This involves laminating procedures discussed in chapter 6. Many pieces of furniture are the result of both approaches and determining the best method for achieving the form utilizes knowledge of all the techniques.

In this chapter the emphasis is on furniture created essentially from a log or board, from prelaminated pieces of wood and from simple laminates.

The craftsman who can produce a chair, table, cradle, and the range of objects illustrated, from a piece of rough, dried log, has to be able to visualize that form within the log. He begins, as does the sculptor, by carving away, or subtracting, the wood, using saws, chisels, gouges, and mallets, until he releases the form he visualizes. If he carves away too much, or encounters a defect within the log, he may have to revise his vision and alter his design as he works. It is difficult to develop a form from a log and adhere to a strict design or a preconceived drawing as to the appearance of the final piece. Problems within the log, defects, checks, etc., may necessitate revision as the work progresses; one must also take into account the balance and the comfort of the piece.

Sterling King's unusually sensitive forms carved from huge walnut stumps utilize the natural protrusions and growth of the log. His large pieces are created essentially by direct carving. You'll note these protrusions particularly in his table with the deep check; the check becomes a dominant design feature using the texture and tactile quality of the wood and combining a smooth and rough finish where

CHAIR. Lawrence B. Hunter. 34 inches high, 26 inches
wide, 34 inches deep. Carved from a log of black walnut
and English walnut.

necessary. The only additions he may use in his log forms are soft leather for comfort
in the chairs and a steam-bent base as a stand for a tabletop.

Robert C. Whitley's work exhibits his depth of respect and sensitivity for the
woods he uses. Whitley often combines the rough natural outer edge shape of a slab
of wood cut from a log with a harmoniously carved smooth shape in the supporting
legs when the slab is used for a table or desk (page 76).

Most craftsmen will not have ready access to large root forms, logs, and slabs
of rough walnut, so the approach used by Robert Dice in creating a rocking chair is
practical for the beginning furniture maker to become familiar with the methods for
building up simple shapes and carving them to achieve a sculptural, smooth-flowing
form. The approach can be used for chairs with legs as well as for rocking chairs.
The challenge of creating a rocking chair is great because it poses problems in kinetic
structuring; the rocker member must be curved and the chair balanced so it will
remain in the position desired.

In contemporary furniture, heights of chair seats, backs, and so forth are
optional. Commercial furniture manufacturers have charts showing the most com-

CHAIR. Jon Brooks. 31 inches high. Elm. Direct carving of a log utilizes the organic form of nature to make the object one with the needs of man. *Courtesy, artist*

fortable heights for chairs and angles of tilts for backs when chairs are to be used for desks, dining, lounging, etc. The same is true for table heights. The craftsman may wish to adhere to some of these standardized measures (see Appendix), and may have to do so if he is creating a special design for a commission or for a particular purpose in an office, a dining room, or for a certain client who requires a customized piece of furniture. The craftsman who is making a design for himself, or utilizing the materials available, may permit the materials to dictate size; a small log may evolve into a low tilted chair that is comfortable for lounging; a large log may have a high seat and suggest a throne.

Generally, the tools and methods of joinery shown in previous chapters are applied to the directly carved furniture piece, depending upon the problems to be solved. In addition, one may require hand gouges which are driven with a lignum vitae mallet usually found in a sculptor's studio. Gouges and chisels are available in shapes from the curved U to sharp V and in different blade widths to permit carving in tiny and wide areas.

Rasps, files, and scrapers are used for blending large areas of a form and for smoothing surfaces, particularly in hardwoods that will be sandpapered and polished. Files tend to leave deep marks in softwood; rasps and files are made in flat, round, half-round and other shapes. A Surform tool is indispensable because it cuts clean and does not tear the wood. Rifflers are small files and rasps that are curved and tapered at each end and used for working in awkward corners and rounded areas.

LORD'S BENCH. Dempsey R. Calhoun. 2 feet high, 8 feet wide, 1½ feet deep. Hand-carved walnut with pegging details in legs. The natural check is utilized as part of the form. *Below:* Detail. *Collection and photo, Mint Museum of Art, Charlotte, N.C.*

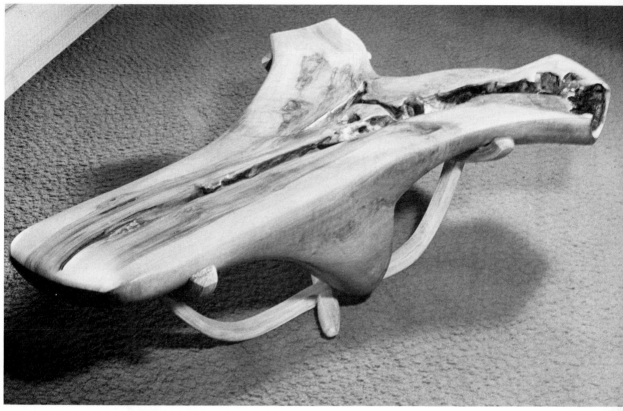

COCKTAIL TABLE. Sterling King. 15 inches high, 54 inches wide, 36 inches deep. The actual shape of the English walnut trunk section dictated the form. The white oak carriage is steam bent. The result of a decayed heartwood area becomes an integral part of the design and a contrasting texture to the sanded smooth surfaces.

Below: View of opposite end also showing detail of interior area.

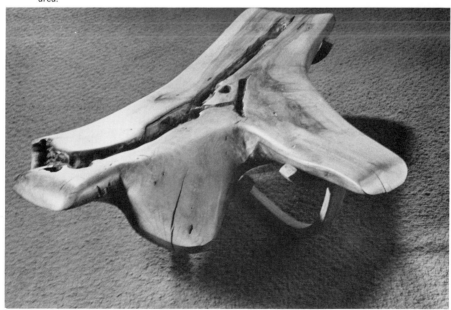

Sterling King's furniture pieces exhibit a pure and sensitive approach to the use of the natural organic forms of a log. Nature has placed compound planes on the logs that Sterling King selects and he must meticulously study these planes before he knows the form he wishes to release. As he carves he continually reevaluates the shapes in relation to one another, and to space. He reshapes some areas greatly to achieve a harmonious sculptural interplay of parts that still appear natural. Ultimately, the piece must be functional as well as sculptural. He uses what is within nature so it retains an interaction with nature; it is a different approach from beginning with a cylindrical log and carving.

Sterling King's raw material for a drawer stand is the root formation of an English walnut tree he has unearthed an allowed to cure. He may work on several pieces at a time going from one to another as he feels the forms emerg

At right: The drawer detail exhibits the careful attention detail by the designer. He has emulated the pattern of woodworm by carefully re-creating the natural texture wit a high-speed grinder.

THE DRAWER STAND (before final finishing). Sterling King 38 inches high, 60 inches wide, 14 inches deep. Englis walnut. The drawer has been carefully excised from the lc and fits perfectly. The front retains the natural carve planes of the log. Protrusions of the root, below the artist arm, are retained and integrated into the design.

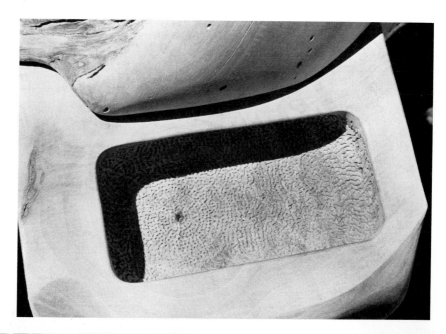

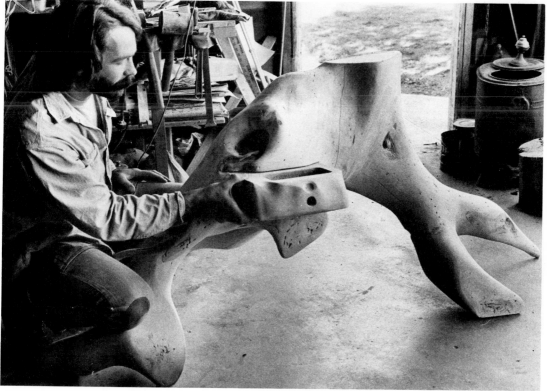

Opposite, top: Side view.

Opposite, bottom: Detail of side and back portion with stuffed suede forms protruding through the negative spaces.

SEATING PIECE. Sterling King. 4½ feet high, approximately 4½ feet diameter, seat, 20 inches deep. California black walnut with suede.

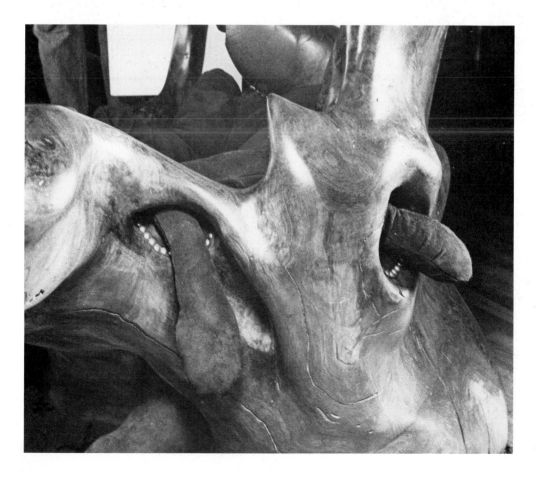

SEATING PIECE. Sterling King. 32 inches high, 44 inches wide, 48 inches deep. California black walnut. Leather upholstery over rubberized hair and Dacron padding. The cut leather edge is rolled and tacked.

Opposite, top: SIDE ROCKER. Sterling King. 54 inches high, 42 inches wide, 19 inches deep. English walnut with top grain finished leather.

Opposite, bottom: OTTOMAN. Sterling King. 15 inches high, 32 inches wide, 28 inches deep. Black walnut with top grain finished leather.

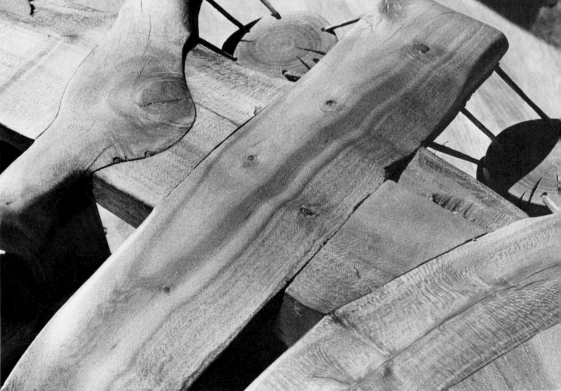

TABLE AND BENCHES. Sterling King. Table, 29 inches high, 60 inches wide, 32 inches deep. Benches, 19 inches high, 26 inches wide, 23 inches deep. Laminated boards assembled with pegging. The legs have carved organic shapes similar to those the craftsman develops in the root forms.

Opposite, top: TABLE WITH SUSPENDED COASTERS. Sterling King. 14 inches high, 44 inches wide, 19 inches deep. Australian Hakea wood. The round coasters cut from the log are suspended from the horizontal inlays with leather thongs.

Opposite, bottom: Detail.

89

DESIGNER'S CADDY. Tom Bendon. 30 inches high. Red oak with pau ferro wood drawer fronts *(two views)*. The sculptured legs are combined with rounded drawer edges and drawer fronts. Supports are pegged to the drawers. *Photo, artist*

ROCKER. Robert Dice. 36 inches high, 29 inches wide, 36 inches deep. Birch plywood and dowels *(front and back views).* A rocker is a valid design for a beginning furniture-making project. It can be created with easily available materials and inexpensive tools. Many design variations are possible. One can vary the shape of the side members, the height of the back and the width of the dowels. *Collection, Lawrence Hunter*

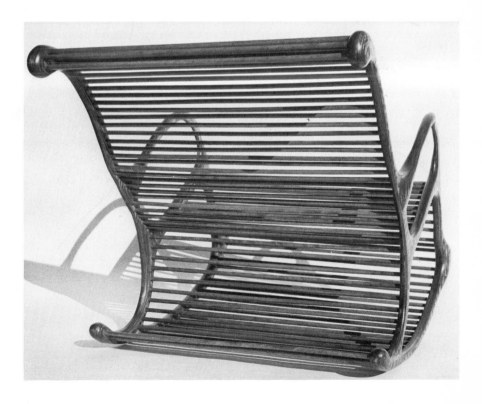

MAKING A DOWEL ROCKER

The following series showing how to create a dowel rocker was developed by Robert Dice and photographed by Lawrence Hunter. In planning a rocker, the curvature and position of the base are important.

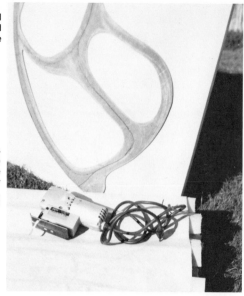

MATERIALS:

Two sheets of Finland birth plywood ¾ inch thick. (This plywood is composed of 17 layers of solid birch per inch.) Approximately seventy ½-inch-diameter birch dowels are cut to the length needed for the final size of the chair desired. You will require a saber saw, drill, rasp, clamps, and a template made of ⅛ inch Masonite, sandpaper, and oil finishes.

CUTTING:

The wood should be placed on a cutting surface such as Styrofoam or canvas with 2-inch-thick strips of Ethafoam (Dow Chemical). This makes the job easier by providing a supporting surface for the plywood and prevents the saber saw from striking a hard undersurface. Markings on the template will be transferred to the plywood to indicate dowel positions.

The plywood is laid out on the cutting surface with the template. Extra shapes are cut out and added to the rocker's frame at the center, base rung, and top on the inside and out. (See clamping setup.) These pieces are used to build up thickness where additional shaping and sculpturing will be accomplished.

The saber saw permits inside cutting. Extra pieces used for the buildup are cut out from the negative areas of the side pieces to conserve and utilize all pieces of the wood.

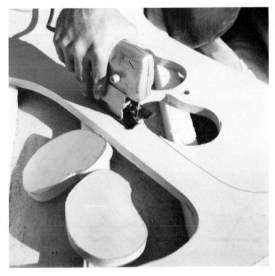

Several pieces have been cut. Strips of soft Ethafoam keep the plywood raised to allow room for the saw blade. The foam cuts easily and does not damage the blade.

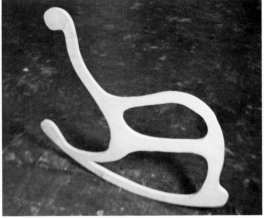

Shape of the plywood side piece; two of these will be needed.

CLAMPING

The first stacked layers are clamped together for positioning.

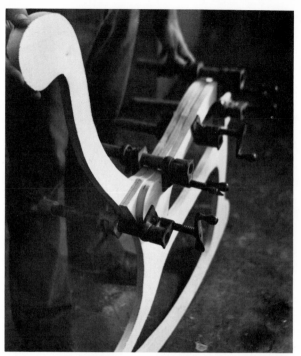

Then both sides of the rocker are clamped up; this keeps the two halves flat and allows a visual check for positioning the layers in matching areas. Spacer blocks are placed at the front at seat level.

The pieces are glued and clamped until dry.

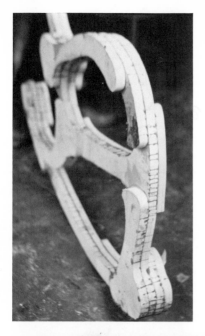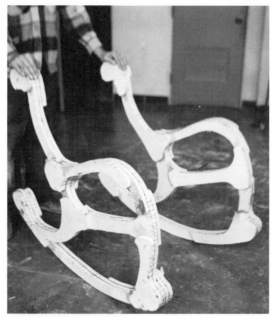

Above, left: This shows the placement of the extra pieces on each side of the frame which will allow the in and out shaping later.

DRILLING THE DOWEL HOLES

Both halves and the template are taped together for marking the dowel positions.

Both halves are still taped together to ensure that the dowel holes are properly aligned and straight. They are drilled simultaneously.

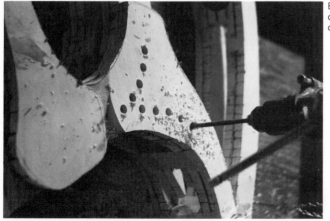

SHAPING

Above, left: General shaping is accomplished first with a Surform® file.

Above, center: Finer shaping and surface smoothing is done with a hand file. Next sand with 80 grit and 120 garnet sandpaper.

Above, right: Mr. Dice begins to insert the dowels into the holes in both sides of the rocker.

Below, left: Next, a drill hole is made in the top surface above each dowel so a small cross dowel can be inserted which will lock the horizontal dowel in place. The cross dowels are made of 5/16 inch diameter birch.

Below, center: The dowel is cut to the proper length, fitted and pounded into place with a mallet. It will be smoothed with files and sandpapers so it is flush with the surface.

Below, right: The excess horizontal dowel is sawed off. The entire rocker is sanded with successively finer garnet papers usually ending with about #220. Finishing, included oiling with dark Watco's Danish Oil; then wet sanding with #400 Silicon carbide sandpaper and reoiling. *Photo series, Lawrence Hunter*

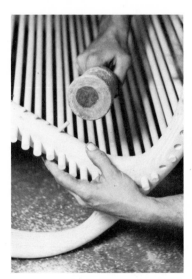

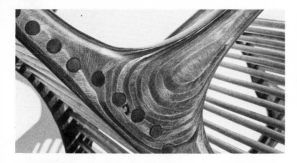

Top: Details of rocker show the arm buildup after it has been shaped, and the doweling.

Bottom: Inner arm shaping and dowels inserted from the inside.

HIGHBACK ROCKER. Robert Dice. The shape of the rocker, height, width, and dimensions of the side pieces can be varied infinitely. *Photo, Lawrence Hunter*

CRADLE. Jack Inhofe. 18 inches high, 25 inches wide, 25 inches deep. Oak, and rosewood with cotton cord. Unusual joinery techniques are illustrated in the details, below. Each spindle moves within its pegging holes. *Collection, Lawrence Hunter*

Detail of cradle left. Knotted and wrapped cord provide lightness and rough texture to the smooth woods.

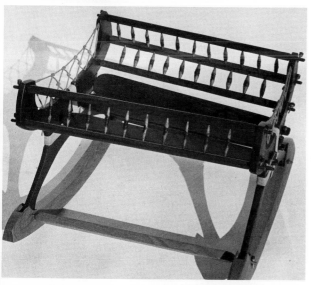

Detail of cradle above. Removable pegs secure the exposed tenon; all are hand carved.

PEOPLE CHAIRS. Robert Dice. 50 inches high, 23 inches wide, 24 inches deep. Fir laminated and carved.

HEADBOARD. Robert Dice. 6 feet high, 4 feet wide, 3½ inches deep. Fir with carved figures.

LOVE SEAT. Robert Dice. 30 inches high, 64 inches wide, 19 inches deep. Fir with walnut stain. Glued sections and carving. *All pieces, collection, David P. Wiles, San Diego, Calif.*

ROCKING CHAIR. Robert C. Whitley. American black walnut. The artist has combined a simple but fluid, graceful design with structural strength and durability and the need for comfort. The result is a functional and sculptural chair. *Photos, artist*

ROBERT C. WHITLEY CREATES A ROCKER

The following series demonstrates the development of the rocking chair and the working methods of Robert C. Whitley. The photos were taken by Robert C. Whitley III.

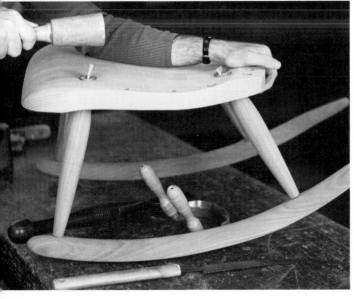

The chair utilizes the joining, carving, and assembling techniques already demonstrated. The spindles are bent by steam bending (see chapter 6). Each spindle is gracefully tapered for the back of the rocking chair. Tapering at the top provides tensile flexibility for comfort as well as esthetics. The subtle curvature of the seat conforms to the shape of the body. It is shaped with the double-handled tool beneath the rocker, called an "inshave." The curved blade is placed on the wood and drawn toward the body across the seat with a regular pressure and pull. The leg tops are kerf-sawn and wedges are driven into them with a lignum vitae mallet. The wedge forces and expands the wood of the leg against the sides of its complementary hole in the seat, making a secure and permanent joint.

A tension saw is used to trim off the excess wedge used in the leg-seat joint. The saw cuts on the pull position; its narrow shape and positioning of its teeth allow great accuracy for cutting small pieces in hard-to-get-at places. Holes have already been made in the seat for the back and arm spindles.

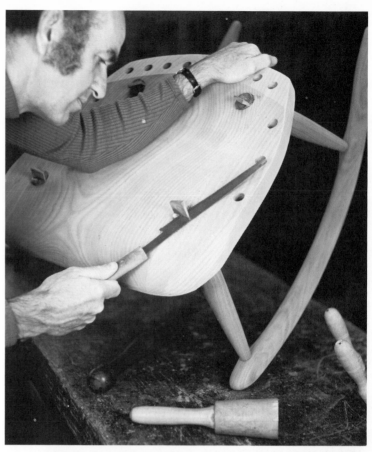

The tapered back spindles have been bent by the steaming process. They are hammered into prepared holes at the back of the seat.

The back spindles are crowned with a steamed and shaped rail. The positioning of the receptive holes in the cresting rail is such that slight tension is effected on the spindles as they are snapped into place which creates a tight and secure fit without use of nails, screws, or pegs.

Bottom, left: The arm spindles are kerf-sawn in preparation for the wedging that will hold the chair arm to the side spindles. The back end of each arm is shaped and fitted to embrace the end spindles of the back. This structure adds stability to the arms and yields a clean visual structural line.

Bottom, right: The wedge is hammered into the kerf-sawn arm spindles that have been inserted into the arms. The excess wedge will be sawn off and finished as in the seat and leg spindles. The joint fulfills the requirements of strength, a smooth surface and esthetic repeat details. The wood is finished by oiling and hand rubbing. Refer to the finished rocker on page 100 and to Mr. Whitley's finishing methods, page 75.

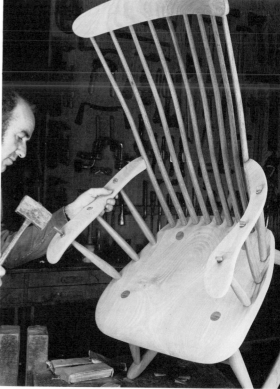

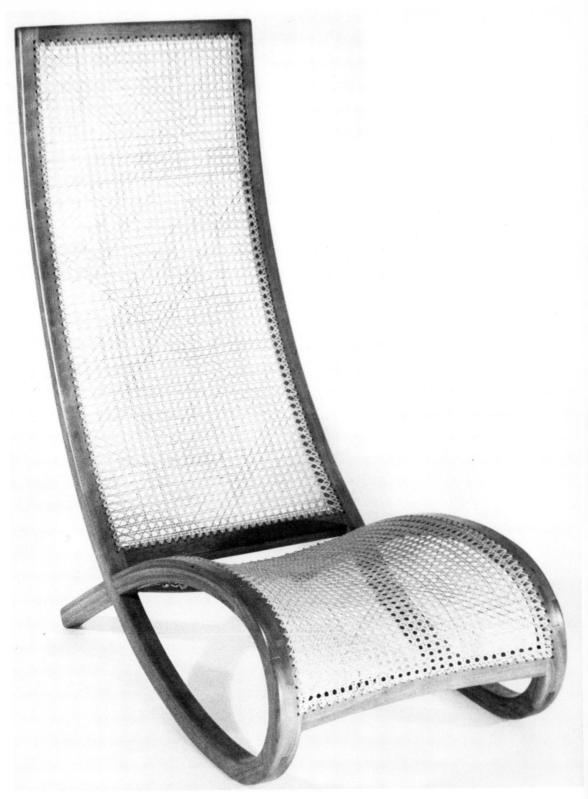

CANED CHAIR. William C. Leete. Laminated black cherry
with hand-caned seat and back. *Courtesy, artist*

ROCKING CHAIR. Edward G. Livingston. 42 inches high, 24 inches wide, 39 inches deep. Teak with laminated, hand-carved and bent portions. *Courtesy, Sterling Associates, Palo Alto, Calif.*

ROCKER. Ann Malmlund. 46 inches high, 44 inches long.
Redwood. Pieces are laminated, carved, and joined with
pegging.

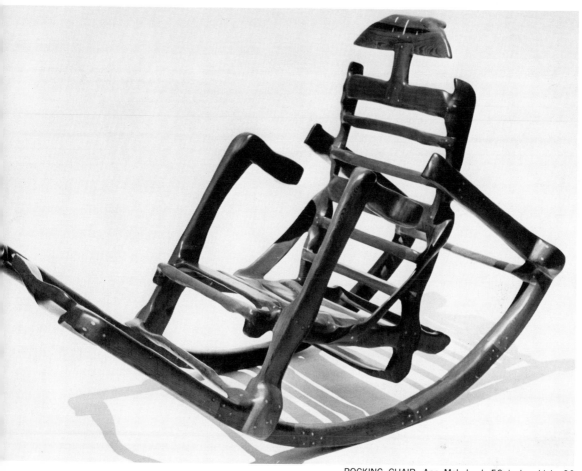

ROCKING CHAIR. Ann Malmlund. 50 inches high, 32 inches wide, 62 inches long. Both chairs offer a completely different design style and approach to a rocker than those presented in the preceding pages. Ms. Malmlund's work often approaches fantasy forms (see additional pieces in chapter 8). *Photo, Tom Tramel*

In this series, Mr. Whitley demonstrates additional techniques and working procedures for creating a chair. His handcrafted American black walnut armchair has simple, graceful lines that will blend with any decorating scheme. The hand-sculpted seat, cresting rail, and arms are designed for comfort, yet they state an integration of visual lines. *Photo, Robert C. Whitley. The following series of demonstration photos is by Robert C. Whitley III.*

The shape of the spindles for the armchair are hand planed into perfectly duplicated shapes by the use of a jig which the artist devised for this purpose. The jig has a negative shape of one side of the spindle; when the spindle is placed in the shape, the top surface is planed so all the spindles are the same shape.

The ends of the spindles are further tapered with a finer plane to fit precisely into the holes in the seat and cresting rail at the chair top. These two hole sizes are perfectly represented in the holes drilled in the block of wood to the left of the artist which is used to test the spindles' fit.

The curved chair arm is composed of three pieces of solid walnut chosen so that the grain follows the curve. Ends are carefully measured so a perfect joint can be accomplished.

When the three pieces fit perfectly they are glued

. . . and clamped into position until dry.

Holes are drilled in the armpiece for receiving the back and arm support spindles of the chair. The slanted drilling table has been purposely fashioned by the artist so that the holes are drilled at the exact angle necessary to receive the spindles, an angling that is essential for the comfortable slanting of the chair.

Whitley uses a drawknife to shape and sculpt the drilled chair arm roughly. Fine shaping and sculpting are done with a large chisel, two sizes of rasps, and a spoke shave.

The cresting rail for the top of the spindles is also shaped with a drawknife. At the back, you can see how the arm member is clamped while the glue dries.

The spindles have been placed in the seat and now the chair arm is fitted down over the back spindles. The legs are not attached with kerf-sawn joints as in the rocking chair; they are fitted into holes on the seat bottom.

The arm support spindles are kerf-sawn so that when they are fitted through the arm holes, wedges can be driven into the grooves to spread the spindle against the arm hole for a secure joint. The wedge is then sawed and smoothed for detailing and design interest.

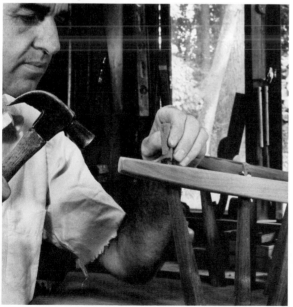

The hand-shaped cresting rail is fitted over the spindle tops. The receiving holes in the rail are spaced to produce a slight tension on the spindles as they are snapped into place; this adds great strength to the entire chair back.

BOARDROOM TABLE AND CHAIRS. Robert C. Whitley. Tabletop made of two edge-glued matching figured walnut boards. Chairs had to be rugged enough to withstand moving by janitors and large enough to seat generously proportioned men. The chairs can be used with or without cushions. *Photo, artist*

EDGE GLUING AND JOINING

Stock boards are not always available in the widths required for large tables. Often grain patterns have to be matched or the pattern in one board may be used to create a different design by joining it with another board. For these procedures, the edges of the board are joined in a process referred to as "edge gluing." The edges of the boards are joined using the same techniques as one uses when laminating the faces of boards. Edge gluing is also used where protrusions and odd shapes may be desired.

DINING ROOM FURNITURE designed and created by Robert C. Whitley: trestle table of three matching boards of Kentucky coffee bean wood is mated with walnut chairs. Two bench tops of 3-inch Kentucky coffee bean wood are tied together with large butterfly dovetails. Wall hung walnut cabinets contain drawers and shelves. At left, top, a sculptured good luck bird, made by the artist, watches over the scene.

The edges to be joined are carefully planed and squared, then glued and clamped. Joinery techniques may be employed and these may or may not be visible. In the photos, page 114, a groove and spline joint provides added strength for the large slabs of wood. Edge joining is used for small boards as well as large slabs. The materials and the particular problem to be solved in construction will dictate the need for a particular process.

A demonstration showing how the trestle table on the preceding page is constructed follows. *Home of J. Burwell Harrison, Princeton, N.J. Photo, artist*

Robert C. Whitley measures a 24-inch-wide, 1½-inch-thick American walnut board for a trestle tabletop. Such board sizes are rare and not commercially available. Whitley has collected these boards over the years by cutting down trees and curing the boards for six years out of doors and three years indoors in a specially heated building.

The wood slab is being edge-joined. This process squares off the board edge to remove any irregularities in the edge surface and to prepare it for joining with another such board for a large tabletop. After the machine joining is finished, additional work must be accomplished with hand planes to ensure an exact fit.

A router is used to make a groove in the edge of each board to be joined. Another strip of wood, called a spline, is carefully hand-planed and fitted to fill the grooves in each board edge when they are butted against each other. The spline is glued between the two boards resulting in an extremely strong mortise and tenon joint.

The pair of routed and splined matching boards are glued together and clamped until dry. When the clamps are removed, the tabletop will be planed and sanded by hand to remove any tactile differentiations of the surface where the joint occurs.

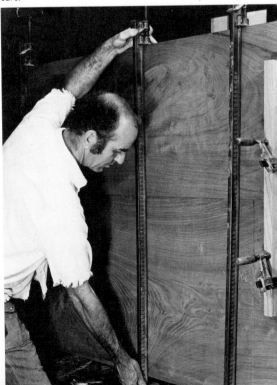

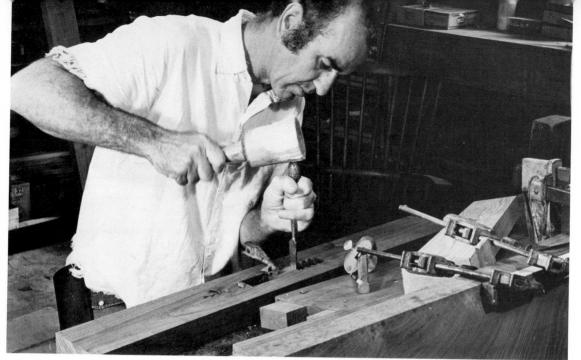

The supporting base member of the trestle table is being mortised to receive the tenon leg section. The square mortise holes are first roughed out with a drill press, then meticulously finished by hand with a mallet and chisels.

The trestle part of the table base is fitted into the leg members. This mortise and tenon joint is extremely strong and practically indestructible. *Photo series, Robert C. Whitley III*

DINING SET. Dan Wenger. Redwood slab tabletop made of edge-glued boards set on a frame of welded steel that has been painted flat black, burnished to a high luster, and coated with polyurethane. Chairs are latigo leather with steel. *Courtesy, artist*

CONFERENCE CHAIR AND BUTTERFLY TABLE. Robert C.
Whitley. The creamy colored sapwood of the walnut tree is
incorporated in the tabletop design wood joinings. The
chair seat slants down for comfort; it can be used with or
without cushions. *Photo, artist*

HUNT BOARD TABLE. Frances F. Jones. 30 inches high, 30 inches wide. Walnut with ceramic mosaic inlays. Much of the structure consists of glued-up small pieces of wood as large pieces were not available to the artist. Hand-rubbed varnish finish. *Collection, Dr. and Mrs. Clarence Shaw, Tenn. Photo, Hinkle Studios*

COFFEE TABLE. Hal E. Davis. 18 inches high, 48 inches wide. Bird's-eye maple. *Collection, Memphis Hardwood Lumberman's Assoc. Courtesy, artist*

LAMINATIONS. Jack Rogers Hopkins. *Front:* Chair and coffee table (half detail). Black walnut and birch veneer. *Center:* Cherrywood chair. *Rear:* Edition chair in Finnish birch plywood. *Courtesy, artist*

ARK. William A. Keyser. 90 inches high, 73 inches wide, 36 inches deep. Teak. Steam bent and barrel stave construction. *Courtesy, artist*

CHEST-TABLE AND BENCH. Federico Armijo. Bedroom pieces from a complete interior design "La Familia." *Courtesy, artist*

COFFEE TABLE. Tommy Simpson. 28 inches high. Pine with acrylic. Fantasy shapes with a painted surface. *Courtesy, artist*

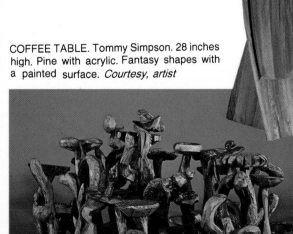

PAIR OF DOORS. Federico Armijo. Each 84 inches
high, 36 inches wide. Oak. *Photo, Dick Kent*

SEA ANEMONE. Lawrence B. Hunter. Fabric over urethane foam. *Courtesy, artist*

SEAT. James Danisch. 15 inches high. Stoneware.
Courtesy, artist

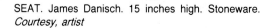

TABLE. Jon Brooks. 19 inches high. Elmwood. Direct carving with detailed joinery. *Courtesy, artist*

CRADLE. Jack Rogers Hopkins. 4 feet high, 3 feet wide, 4 feet deep. Cherry, wormy chestnut, and rosewood. Laminated and hand carved. *Courtesy, artist*

STORAGE UNIT. John Makepeace. Laminated birch, acrylics, and stainless steel. *Courtesy, © John Makepeace*

JAW CHAIR. Mark Abrahamson. 40 inches high, 54 inches wide, 68 inches long. Plywood, wire, newspaper, papier-mâché, and fiberglass. *Photo, Larry Hunter*

SEATING UNITS. Robert Olsen. Urethane foam with stretch fabric covering. Pieces can be rearranged for seating, sleeping, lounging. *Courtesy, artist*

DESK. Ann Malmlund. 56 inches high, 29 inches wide, 13 inches deep. Redwood. Fantasy cabinetry with myriad carved inner compartments. *Courtesy, artist*

DESK. Robert C. Whitley. 75 inches long, 44 inches wide. Highly figured walnut slab top with drawers on wide leg base. *Collection, Colonel Thomas E. Bass, Washington, D.C.; Photo, Jack Venetone*

PAIR OF DOORS. Svetozar Radakovitch. Fiberglass coating over wood. *Courtesy, artist*

Table on lathe. Stephen Hogbin. Table piece
over 6 feet in diameter has cardboard laminated
so turned parts can be removed to create
smaller table (*front*). *Courtesy, artist*

CHICKEN CHAIRS. John Bauer. Rooster: oak and shedua. Hen: oak. Edge and stacked laminations. *Courtesy, artist*

Center:
WOMB ROOM. Jack Rogers Hopkins. 6 feet high, 9 feet wide, 13 feet deep. Honduras mahogany, ash, and ebony stacked laminations. *Courtesy, artist*

Bottom:
TUBE CHAIR. Sterling King. Inner tube and binding strap. *Photo, Larry Hunter*

DESK AND CHAIR. Al Lockwood. 29 inches high, 72 inches wide, 48 inches deep. Honduras mahogany. Stacked lamination machine and hand carved. *Courtesy, artist*

EIGHT-HARNESS LOOM AND BENCH. Dennis M. Morinaka. 34 inches high, 68 inches wide, 35 inches deep. Eastern maple, vermilion, Cambodian narra, Finnish birch, Brazilian rosewood, and oak. Bench, 22 inches high, has three covered compartments. *Courtesy, artist*

COFFEE TABLE. Edward Jajosky. 18 inches high. Made from three pieces of mahogany which were hand sculptured. *Courtesy, artist*

TYPING TABLE. Edward Jajosky. 25¾ inches high, 40 inches wide, 20 inches deep. Walnut. *Courtesy, artist*

CONFERENCE TABLE AND CHAIRS. Michael Bock. Walnut
and leather. *Courtesy, artist*

Opposite, top left: END TABLE. Robert C. Whitley. 22
inches high. Creamy colored sapwood of the walnut tree.
Photo, artist

Opposite, top right: BOOMERANG CHAIR. Robert C. Whitley. 31 inches high, 21 inches wide, 23 inches deep. A
multiple-purpose, lightweight design. *Photo, artist*

Opposite, bottom: FOOTSTOOL. James Nash. 12 inches
high, 17 inches wide, 15 inches deep. White oak. Top is
padded and upholstered. *Courtesy, artist*

GAME TABLE. Federico Armijo. 27 inches high, 72 inches
wide, 20 inches deep. American black walnut. Two views.
Courtesy, artist

FOUR CHAIRS. Clarence Teed. The third chair from left is walnut and cherry: all others are walnut. *Courtesy, artist*

DISPLAY CASE. Donald Lloyd McKinley. 60 inches wide. Top is carved stacked lamination with the curved glass from a 1954 Plymouth rear window across the top. *Photo, artist*

ADJUSTABLE CHAIR. James Nash. 50 inches high, 28 inches wide, 27 inches deep. Koa wood and leather. The chair can be tilted back to different positions.

Opposite, right: details of the various types of joints used. *Courtesy, artist*

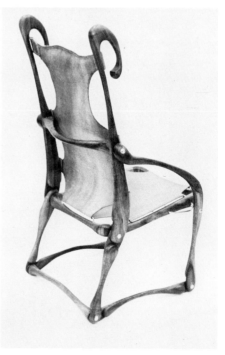

Four tables by Roger Thompson utilize sculptural techniques in different approaches, materials and solutions. *All photos, Domenica Thompson*

Thick mahogany boards glued and shaped. Table may be set on end and used as a freestanding sculpture. 16 inches high, 5½ feet wide, 3 feet deep.

Thin oak boards shaped with the top pegged to the three legs. 32 inches wide, 21 inches deep.

Red Mahogany. 16 inches high, 5 feet wide, 4 feet deep.
Various sized wood blocks assembled by gluing and pegging with hickory dowels for color contrast.

Odd-shaped walnut wood blocks have been cut and
smoothed where necessary and assembled with concrete
grouting. 16 inches high, 5 feet wide, 3 feet deep.

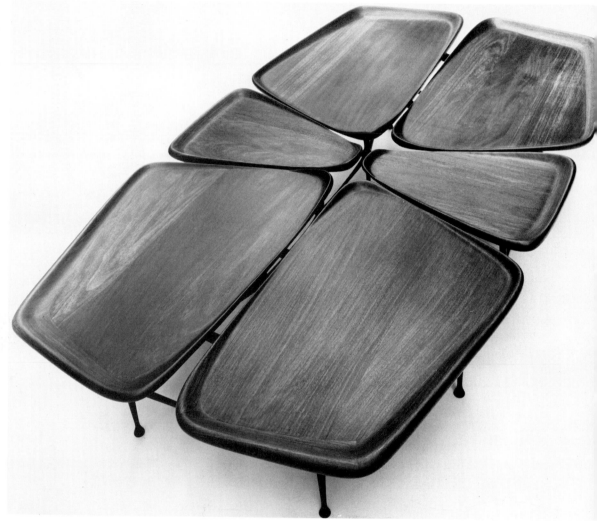

TABLE WITH SEGMENTED TOP. Tom Tramel. 6 feet wide, 42 inches deep. East Indian rosewood and ebony. The molded forms of the top are bound and supported by a spidery framework of legs, each shaped and molded with complex precision and detailing. *Courtesy, Pasadena Museum of Art, Calif.*

LAW TABLE. Joe Barano *(two views)*. 16 inches high, 48 inches wide, 26 inches deep. African Padouk wood. A marvelous interplay of sculptural forms beneath, through and on top of the table. *Photo, Tom Tramel*

CAPTAIN'S CHAIR. Edward Jajosky. 28 inches high, 26 inches wide, 23 inches deep. Laminated oak crest rail with laminated plywood legs with oak veneer. Black leather seat stretched over a wood frame and tied with rope through holes with grommets on the underside. *Courtesy, artist*

CANTILEVERED CHAIR. Donald Lloyd McKinley. 30½ inches high, 21¾ inches wide, 24 inches deep. Laminated birch with black cotton lacing. *Collection, H. and L. Helwig, Ontario, Canada. Photo, artist*

STRAP CHAIR. Douglas Blimker *(two views)*. Zebrawood and leather. *Photo, Tom Tramel*

MIRROR STAND. Bud Tullis. Exquisitely hand carved detailing that follows and utilizes the natural wood designs. *Courtesy, artist*

MUSIC STAND. Tom Tramel. 48 inches high, 26 inches wide, 24 inches deep. Walnut. Four individually shaped forms are held together by sculptured wood joinings beneath. *Photo, Tom Tramel*

STANDING MIRROR. Terry A. Smith. 7 feet high. Rosewood with a bronze mirror.

MUSIC STAND FOR DUETS. Terry A. Smith. 5 feet high. Goncalo alves, rosewood, and brass parts. *Courtesy, artist*

Opposite: COAT TREE AND LOUNGE CHAIR. Edward G. Livingston. Tree: 72 inches high, 13 inches square at base. Chair: 50 inches high, 36 inches wide, 26 inches deep. Both pieces made of American black walnut. Signed and numbered. *Courtesy, Sterling Associates, Palo Alto, Calif.*

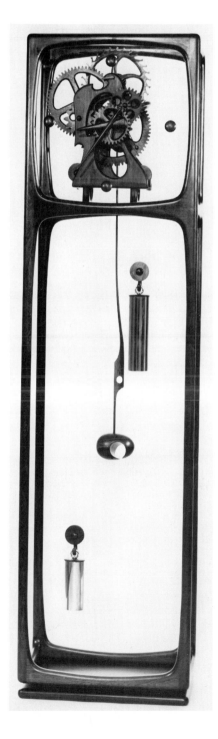

CLOCK. Lawrence B. Hunter. The concept of the hand carved escapement suggests a fanciful animal whose head moves very slowly back and forth.

Left: GRANDFATHER CLOCK. John Gaughan. 6 feet high, 18 inches wide, 12 inches deep. All Brazilian rosewood. Handcarved gears. Brass weights. *Courtesy, Sterling Associates, Palo Alto, Calif.*

135

WOMB ROOM. Jack Rogers Hopkins. 6 feet high, 13 feet wide, 9 feet deep. Stacked lamination of Honduras mahogany, ash and ebony. A sound system is incorporated in the unit. *Courtesy, artist*

laminating, turning, bending

6

The shapes and sizes of furniture must often exceed the size of a piece of wood that can be derived from a tree. Commercially cut boards are of standard widths and thicknesses; therefore, gluing one or more boards together is essential for expanding wood surfaces. This gluing method is referred to as "laminating." In addition to expanding the wood surface, it enables the designer to combine one or several kinds of woods, often stacking up layer upon layer and then carving out the form. Laminating is used extensively for wood sculpture because of the grain patterns, colors, and other characteristics each wood lends to the sculptor's surfaces, and the same is true for furniture pieces.

Laminating is not a modern invention; but the modern applications of the technique to sculptural furniture is charting new courses. A recognized innovator of these new forms with wood is Wendell Castle, who believes that furniture should complement nature rather than contrast to it. His furniture pieces usually have an organic reference unlike the constructed forms of more traditionally conceived furniture. They seem to evolve smoothly from a base and flow upward; some begin at the ceiling and are suspended almost surrealistically.

Castle builds up forms from one-inch layers of wood glued and clamped; the work is then carved as if from a solid block, smoothed and finished with many coats of hand-rubbed linseed oil which yields a low luster and keeps highlights to a minimum. Castle, who taught at the School for American Craftsmen of the Rochester Institute of Technology, has passed his thinking and expertise along to many students who then established themselves as professional craftsmen in many areas.

Organically conceived, flowing sculptural laminated forms are carried to exciting heights by Southern California artist Jack Rogers Hopkins. They are achieved by layering and laminating various woods in roughly the general shape of the finished form. The examples illustrated attest to Mr. Hopkins's ability to visualize and create an unending assortment of shapes that are functional and sculpturally exciting.

The process of creating a laminated furniture design involves imagining, planning, and designing the piece. Al Lockwood sketches his ideas or carves miniature models in balsa wood; another artist works out his design in Styrofoam. Lockwood may sketch the piece in three dimensions, and often from different angles, until he is sure of the stress and balance points and feels he has solved any structural problems. Actual size drawings for designs are done on huge pieces of brown paper which he spreads on the floor of his workshop. These drawings detail the number of one-inch layers to be used and how they will be laid up for shaping.

The next step involves selecting the woods to be used and cutting the shapes. For laminating, each surface to be glued must be absolutely flat and smooth. If not, when the glue dries there will be gaps between the layers that cannot be corrected. Gluing up the stacked laminates must be accomplished carefully; some artists do one layer at a time, others glue up the entire piece and then clamp it.

Edge gluing is used to add width to boards or to join bases to tabletops and other members as opposed to stack laminates where the broad faces of the boards are glued. Usually the glue is stronger than the wood; once the piece has been edge-glued properly, the wood is more apt to tear than the joint is to break.

Any of the surfaces of the cut board may be glued; the face, edges, ends, or all three. Joinery details will strengthen the glued parts and are often used as a decorative motif as well, and examples are illustrated. Boards that are cross-grain laminated should be used indoors only; the different movement from wood expansion and contraction can cause cross-grain woods to separate at the glue joints. For furniture, choose select grade boards, quartersawed to minimize warpage.

When the boards have been glued and dried thoroughly, the shaping begins and the tools used depend upon the preference of the sculptor and the amount of carving to be done. Chain saws, routers, and grinders are used for the initial shaping, then finer shaping is accomplished with whatever available tool will do the job. The final steps include sanding and finishing with an oil or other surface finish, depending upon the color and gloss desired.

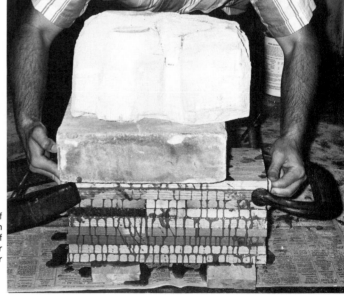

"Stack" laminating permits you to stack layers of different types and colors of wood boards. They can be turned so the grain will differ in various parts of the finished block; some running horizontally and/or vertically. The glued boards must be clamped, or weighted, so the surfaces bond thoroughly.

Prelaminated woods such as birch and plywood are available from lumber dealers. Thin layers of the wood have been glued cross-grained to one another and prepared as board that is sold for a variety of building purposes. Birch can be particularly effective in furniture design when the original laminates are built up in several layers to expand the size of a given area. Shaping and sanding reveal the layers and this procedure is used in a design by Robert Dice, page 98, chapter 5.

Interviewing craftsmen involved in furniture design and observing their studios and working procedures has emphasized the creativity and inventiveness involved, not only in the furniture that results, but in how the many mechanical problems are solved. Perhaps the most astonishing setup was in the garage turned into workshop, and the backyard with a Rube Goldberg-type structure at Jocko Johnson's in Southern California. Most craftsmen work with assorted clamps to glue up their laminates; but Jocko Johnson, with the help of Milon Hutchinson, developed a hydraulic press from improvised materials which is described and illustrated on pages 146 and 147.

Bending wood is an important accompaniment to the laminate process. It often calls for a steaming chamber into which the wood can be placed for softening it. John Snidecor of California State College, Long Beach, demonstrated the unit he developed from an aluminum tank reclaimed from an aircraft salvage yard. He uses the chamber for steaming thin strips of wood which are laminated and bent.

William Keyser of the School for American Craftsmen, Rochester Institute of Technology, New York, works with thick pieces of wood, as opposed to thin laminates, and is able to accomplish subtly bent wood members for his graceful, restrained, and elegant designs.

The ability to laminate and bend woods in a variety of ways extends a craftsman's design possibilities. The processes are not necessarily easy; nor are they accomplished without experimentation, trial, error, and often complete failure. Sometimes, they are never really "perfected." But in the hands of one who has worked with woods in myriad ways and learned many procedures, the potential of the laminated form is a constant challenge.

"Edge" laminating, as opposed to stacked laminating, refers to the process of gluing the edges of the boards to achieve a wider surface. It also requires careful gluing and clamping. Sometimes additional joinery methods are required as shown in Robert C. Whitley's series, page 114. Edge and stacked laminations may be used in the same piece.

Al Lockwood's stacked and glued cut wood shapes are clamped together in stages. The final top boards have been glued and clamped in position. *Below:* He begins to round off the shapes with a hand held chain saw.

Refining the shape is accomplished with gouges and a mallet.

The entire piece must be sanded, working from heavy to fine grades of sandpaper. He usually uses Danish or linseed oil finish, hand rubbed, to bring out the natural grains of the woods. *Photos, courtesy artist*

TABLE. Al Lockwood. 30 inches high, 4 feet wide, 6 feet deep. Philippine mahogany. *Photo, artist*

TABLE AND CHAIRS. John Bauer. Mixed hardwoods laminated then carved. *Courtesy, Sterling Associates, Palo Alto, Calif.*

CONFERENCE TABLE. Milon Hutchinson and Jocko Johnson. Top is 8 feet wide, 4 feet deep. Design and edge-glued slab top is by Milon Hutchinson. The laminated and free-form carved base is by Jocko Johnson. *Courtesy, Milon Hutchinson*

DINING SET. Jocko Johnson. Table, 28 inches high, 60 inches long, 39 inches wide. Walnut. The oval table has a repeat of ovate shapes in the negative areas of the table legs, the cross section and in the matching high- and low-backed chairs. *Courtesy, artist*

COCKTAIL TABLE. Jocko Johnson. 17½ inches high, 61 inches long, 20 inches deep. Black walnut stacked lamination hand carved. *Courtesy, artist*

PULL-UP CHAIR. Jocko Johnson. 34 inches high, seat approximately 14-inch diameter. Mahogany. *Collection, Milon and Mable Hutchinson*

The cocktail table *(left)* evolves from stacked shapes of kiln dried wood and it looks like this as Mr. Johnson prepared it for laminating. The woods are then placed in the press *(see next page)* and glued up one layer at a time with white glue. Shaping begins with a chain saw. When they are close to what Johnson wants he switches to a Dumore #6 Super Flex die grinder with files and burrs. Sanding drums are next used on the Dumore and followed by six hand sanding procedures graduating from 80- to 400-grit paper. The smoothed piece is oiled and hand rubbed with Watco oil.

Jocko Johnson built the hydraulic press for laminating in his backyard at a cost of about four hundred dollars plus the air compressor. It will hold a piece 32 inches × 75 inches × 60 inches. He has tested this unit at 75 tons lift but he uses only about twenty tons when building tables. He uses air pressure mostly but if the compressor unit fails he uses water pressure. The lift pressure is created by inflating three 14-inch fire hoses ingeniously connected and accompanied by platens shown in the following photos. The metal uprights were punched with 1 inch diam. holes every six inches and the crosspieces are 7 inch I beams with ½-inch steel plates on each side held by six ½-inch bolts. They have two 1-inch holes to line up with the 1-inch holes in the uprights. Chrysler wrist pins hold it all together.

Johnson began to build the press by using three lengths of 14-foot fire hose. He welded six 3-inch steel tubing stubs to a steel log manifold; then welded caps on the ends of the log and fittings for both air and water pressure. He slipped the hoses on the stubs and ran them the length of the unit and back again. They were connected then to the log manifold stubs with hose clamps.

146

A platform was built to lay the hose set up on. A wood platen 2 inches X 6 inches X 75 inches sandwiched between 1-inch plywood was placed over the platform. Later (after these photos were taken) he added a ¾-inch maple flooring surface that won't give under pressure and prevents any distorting of the laminate. A top platen was built; this is lifted up to insert the table. It is held down on the work by the metal frame which is shimmed up until there is no clearance. (Small wood spacers are inserted to take up all the clearance.)

When the pressure is applied, the hoses lift the first platen pushing the laminate up toward the top platen. Shown is a table *(upside down)* with four layers glued in position. Only one layer is added at a time.

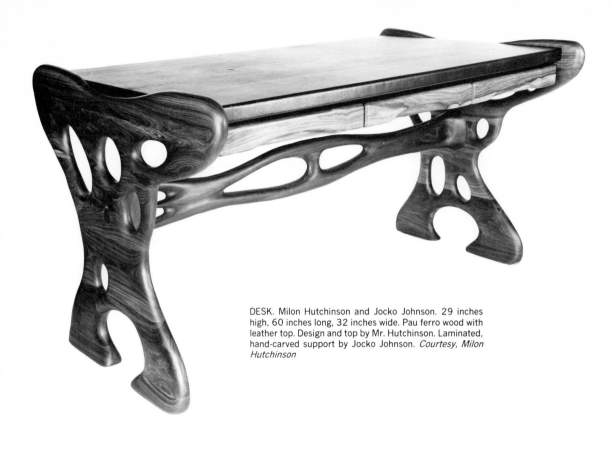

DESK. Milon Hutchinson and Jocko Johnson. 29 inches high, 60 inches long, 32 inches wide. Pau ferro wood with leather top. Design and top by Mr. Hutchinson. Laminated, hand-carved support by Jocko Johnson. *Courtesy, Milon Hutchinson*

COFFEE TABLE. Robert C. Whitley. 66 inches wide, 22 inches deep. Walnut. Laminated and carved base supports a natural-shaped piece of walnut. All boards used in laminating were 2 inches thick. *Collection, Mr. Jack Washburn, New Hope, Pa. Photo, Robert C. Whitley*

COFFEE TABLE. Jack Rogers Hopkins. 16 inches high, 6 feet long, 30 inches wide. Mixed hardwoods. *Courtesy, artist*

BENCH WITH CONTAINER. Bob Falwell. 31 inches high, 101 inches wide, 24 inches deep. Cherrywood. The top of the storage container *(at the left end)* slides around to the back on a pinned hinge.

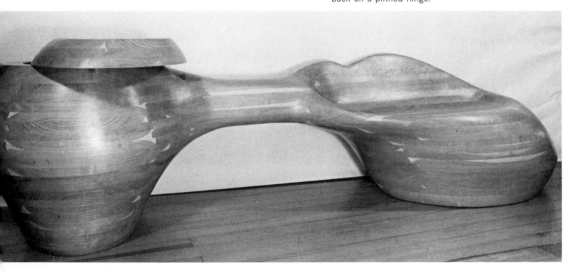

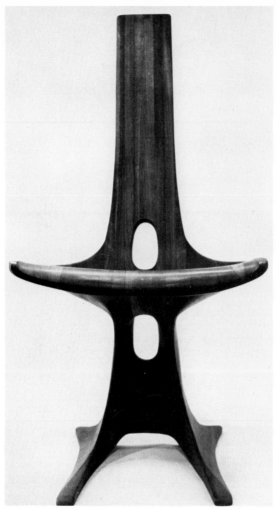

DINING CHAIR. Edward Livingston. American black walnut. *Courtesy, Sterling Associates, Palo Alto, Calif.*

LAMP. Wendell Castle. Laminated woods with an organic design quality; the object appears to grow and evolve upward. *Courtesy, Lee Nordness Gallery, New York*

Opposite: TWO-PIECE CHAIR AND COFFEE TABLE. Jack Rogers Hopkins *(front and back views)*. 4 feet high, 5 feet wide, 30 inches deep. Oak. *Courtesy, artist*

150

EXECUTIVE DESK. Jack Rogers Hopkins. Four views show the three-dimensional quality of the sculptured stacked laminates. 30 inches high, 8 feet wide, 30 inches deep. Black walnut. Made in two sections. The lid on one side raises to hold a telephone box compartment. Spaces are also allowed for desk supplies within the compartment. *Photos, courtesy artist*

DINING TABLE FOR TWO PEOPLE. Jack Rogers Hopkins. Base is 29 inches high, 4 feet wide, 3 feet deep. Laminations consist of shedua (a lamination), teak, maple and birch finished plywood. 3/4-inch plate glass top surface. Chairs are matching woods. Different views of table base and chairs are shown. The interplay of the various wood colors adds to the total sculptural concept. *Collection, Mr. and Mrs. John V. Wise, Oakland, Calif. Photos, Norman Yao*

CHESS TABLE with CHAIRS and CHESSMEN. Jack Rogers
Hopkins. Table: 18 inches high, 36 inches wide, 25 inches
deep. Table and chairs of black walnut and birch. Chess
set: birch veneer, rosewood, padauk, and maple. *Below:*
Frontal view of table and chess pieces.

Opposite: GRANDFATHER'S CLOCK with dining table and
sculpture at rear. Jack Rogers Hopkins. A stunning display
of the virtuosity inherent in the buildup of laminated woods
sculpted by a master artist. *Photos, Norman Yao*

156

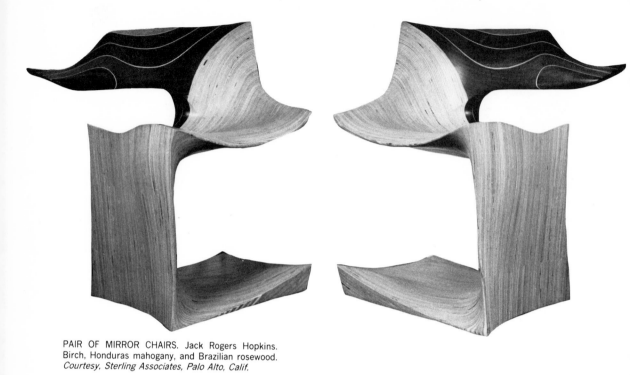

PAIR OF MIRROR CHAIRS. Jack Rogers Hopkins.
Birch, Honduras mahogany, and Brazilian rosewood.
Courtesy, Sterling Associates, Palo Alto, Calif.

TABLE. Tom Lacagnina. 20 inches high, 30 inches
wide, 24 inches deep. *Courtesy, artist*

CHAIR. Hal E. Davis. 24 inches high, 42 inches wide. White oak. *Collection, Mr. Konrad Boazak, Oxford, Miss.*

CHAIR. Hal E. Davis. 28 inches high, 30 inches wide. Pecan. *Collection, Mrs. Charles Teller, Houston, Texas*

LOVE SEAT. James Nash. 17 inches high, 38 inches wide, 17 inches deep. Philippine mahogany. *Below:* Another view showing the positions of the seats in relation to each other.

Opposite: LOUNGE. James Nash. 60 inches high, 84 inches wide, 36 inches deep. Philippine mahogany. *Below:* The artist shows the lounge in use. *Photos, courtesy artist*

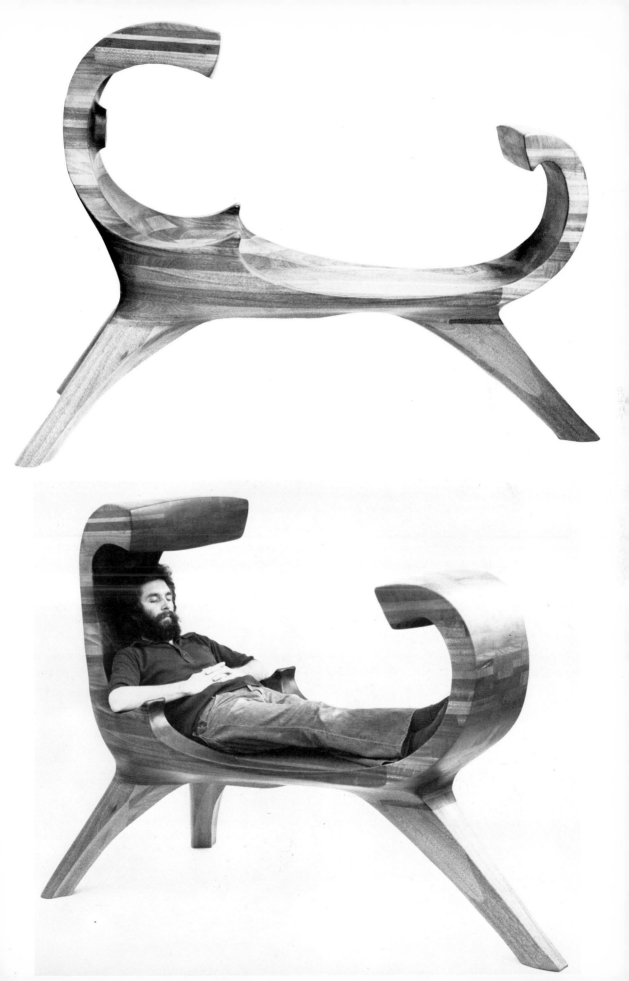

TABLE AND FUR-COVERED CHAIR. Bob Falwell. Table, 28 inches high, 28 inches long, 18 inches wide. Walnut and white oak. Chair is 29 inches high, 23 inches wide, 24 inches deep.

HIGH ROCKER. Carl Gromoll. 42 inches high, 32 inches wide, 28 inches deep. Birch plywood and leather.

SEMICIRCULAR CONVERSATION CHAIR. Carl Gromoll.
43 inches high, 8 feet wide, 4 feet deep. Birch plywood
and leather.

ROCKERS. Carl Gromoll. *(Left)* 25 inches high, 38 inches
wide, 36 inches deep. Birch and spruce plywood and
leather. *(Right)* 45 inches high, 48 inches wide, 36 inches
deep. *Photos, courtesy artist*

CHAIR. Federico Armijo. 36 inches high, 22 inches wide,
20 inches deep. Black walnut. *Courtesy, artist*

TABLE. Tom Lacagnina. 30 inches high, 18-inch cube.
Courtesy, artist

COFFEE TABLE. William A. Keyser. 18 inches high, 51 inches long, 20 inches deep. Zebrawood veneers. End rounded shapes are vacuum formed plywood used with the steam-bending procedure. *Photo, Donald L. Smith*

DESK. Wendell Castle. 29 inches high, 75 inches wide. Cherry. Stacked lamination. *Courtesy, artist*

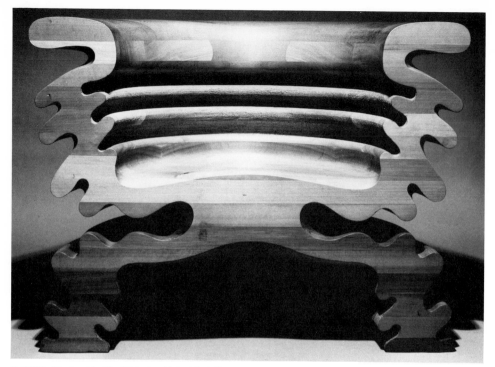

THRONE. Stephen Hogbin. 36 inches high, 4 feet diameter. Cedar. Laminated shape turned on a specially made lathe ending. *Photo, Michel Proux*

Stephen Hogbin, from Ontario, Canada, has developed a unique approach to the lathed form and is stretching the potential of laminated woods by working them on a huge lathe that he improvised from old truck parts and a motor (see demonstration, page 169). To those who think of the lathe for carving small round bowls and containers, and spindles for furniture, Mr. Hogbin's methods can open entirely new horizons. He has kindly shared his technique. His early experiments produced small objects which were fragmented, divided, sectioned, altered, and combined to produce new forms. Eventually, his inventiveness expanded beyond the traditional lathe. He developed a wood-turning device for larger forms made from salvaged pipe, a truck's rear axle and differential turned by a one-horsepower motor. It is these forms, such as the THRONE *(above),* which are furniture pieces or maquettes for furniture. With this unit 3–4-foot edge laminated pieces of wood can be turned for tabletops.

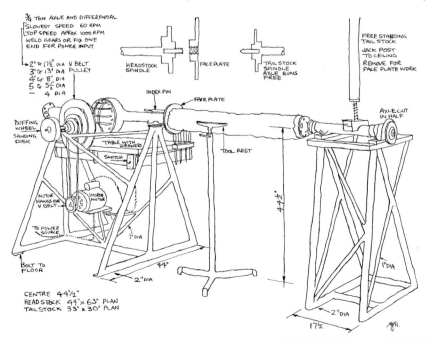

To achieve a divided lathe turned form, Mr. Hogbin laminates two pieces of wood with a cardboard template between them.

Top, left and center: He works the wood from the rear with the usual cutting chisels. The cardboard template is the shape he aims for as he chisels. The wood is mounted on a face plate attached to the improvised lathe.

Top, right: After turning, the two pieces of wood are separated at the cardboard template line . . . first pried apart with a screwdriver . . .

Bottom, left: . . . and, when necessary, separated with a saw.

Bottom, right: A pair, or four, of the turned pieces can be rearranged in infinite combinations. Therefore, the turning is not an end in itself. Rather, it is the basic geometric form that will suggest other design possibilities.

CLAM CHAIR. Edward Jajosky. 26 inches high, 42-inch diameter. Walnut wood and veneer with fur and leather interior *(three views)*. Seating back within chair can be removed or folded down inside the chair to allow closing. Lift-off top portion is adjustable. *Courtesy, artist*

CHAIR–COFFEE TABLE. Jack Rogers Hopkins. 27 inches high, 6 feet wide, 30 inches deep. Maple. *Courtesy, artist*

FOLD-DOWN CHAIR. James Nash. 48 inches high, 32 inches wide, 26 inches deep. Philippine mahogany. Closed and fold-down views. *Courtesy, artist*

SOFA. Robert C. Whitley. 31 inches high, 61 inches long, 32 inches deep. Walnut with crushed velvet cushions mounted on rubber springing. Below, you can see the joining and back shape and the rubber springing of the seat. The ovoid pedestal base gives the form the illusion of floating; but it is rugged and stable. *Collection, Mr. Irving Hoffman, New York, N.Y. Photo, artist*

BISHOP'S CHAIR. Edward Jajosky. 31 inches high, 26½ inches wide, 25½ inches deep. Walnut with maroon velvet cushion. *Courtesy, artist*

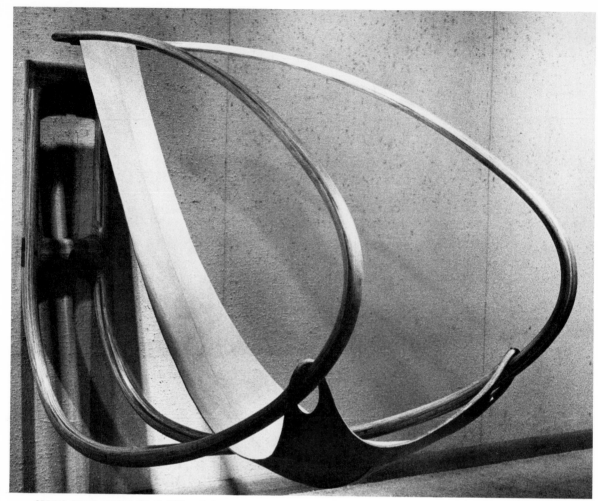

SPRING CHAIR DESIGN NO. 5. William C. Leete. 5 feet high, 30 inches wide, 5½ feet deep. Laminated, bent, and carved red oak with leather. The chair hangs on a wall one foot off the floor. *Courtesy, artist*

BENDING WOOD

Wood bending is an ancient craft known to early civilizations who most often used it to shape timbers into boat hulls. Its first application to modern furniture design, which has had long-lasting influence, was in the now famous rocking chair by the Austrian cabinetmaker, Michael Thonet, in 1860. Thonet had perfected a method of bending solid wood rods into chairs that could be shipped in pieces and then screwed together. Known as bentwood furniture, its curvilinear shapes were primarily in the rococo style. He was granted a patent for the technique and, with his sons, established a network of company showrooms which are still doing a thriving business. His bentwood furniture greatly influenced Alvar Aalto and Marcel Breuer.

Twentieth-century furniture designs continue to rely heavily on bent and curved members in many media. Chrome and some metals require bending in a jig; some have to be heated and shaped by forging. Plastics also require heating and shaping over a jig. Bending wood involves softening it by moistening or steaming, bending it around a jig and clamping it to retain its shape. A molding process used industrially requires a pressure mold machine that works on the same principle as a vacuum form, but it is generally not available to the individual craftsman.

The following demonstrations deal with methods for bending wood that artists have developed without using industrial machinery. They can be adapted to the individual or school workshop.

A *laminating* and clamp-up method for shaping wood is demonstrated by William C. Leete on the following pages. Thin strips of wood cut by a table saw are built up and glued with the grain running parallel to the bend, then clamped around a form to dry. The moisture of the glue may be ample to soften the wood fibers so they are bendable when clamped around a jig. If not, the wood may have to be dampened by sponging with hot water (not immersing it) and allowed to dry while clamped to the form. The form should have a radius slightly less than the required curve to allow for spring-back of the laminated pieces.

When compound curves are required, the jigs and forming must be carefully planned and tested before developing the final piece.

Steam bending can be accomplished on thin and thick pieces of wood. When wood is bent the fibers within the piece must change; those on the inside of the curve are compressed and the fibers on the outer radius are stretched. These stretched outer cells lose strength and result in a weakened piece. Steaming makes these fibers pliable so these changes can be accomplished.

The equipment for steaming may be any kind of improvised chamber (see demonstrations on pages 178 and 182 rigged up so that the wood is suspended in the steam; it should not be immersed in water. The amount of time the wood should remain in the steam depends on its thickness. One hour for each one inch of stock is a suggested rule, but you should allow for experimentation and failure. The maximum temperature should be 230°. If the pressure within the chamber becomes too great, there is a danger of explosion. A flap is placed on an end or in the center of the chamber to keep the pressure from overbuilding. Always bend extra pieces because the bending process may cause some of the stock to split and check.

Hardwoods with long grains such as maple, hickory, oak, elm, walnut, and rosewood may be bent quite easily. Short-grain woods do not bend well. Any wood to be bent should be carefully selected for straight grain parallel to the length of the piece. For relative bendability of woods and additional details refer to: "Bending Solid Wood to Form," a booklet available from the Department of Agriculture, Forest Products Laboratory, P.O. Box 5130, Madison, Wisconsin, 53705.

Forms used for bending laminated wood strips should be patterned in paper first, and then made in wood. Gluing the form to another flat piece of wood makes it easier to clamp around and keep the strips parallel. The height of the mold should be equal to or slightly higher than the wood you are clamping. Pour hot paraffin on the finished mold and scrape off the excess to achieve an easier mold release.

SLEIGH CHAIR. William C. Leete. Chair is 3 feet high, 28 inches wide, 6 feet deep. Laminated and curved red oak strips. Macramé sling. *Courtesy, artist*

The general procedure for creating the bent, springy shapes for his chairs is demonstrated by William Leete.

Depending on the bend desired, several strips are cut on the table saw using uniform widths. They may be ¼ to ⅛ inch thick. Tighter bends require thinner strips. The grain of the strips runs in the same direction. Because the form around which these strips will be curved is so great, Mr. Leete first had to soak the wood in hot water and clamp the strips to the form. Then he glued and reclamped them.

Glue is spread evenly on both surfaces of the strips with a roller.

He quickly clamps the glued-up strips to the form, being careful to keep them even.

The clamping is completed. The strips will be allowed to dry. When removed they will not retain the full bend. They will be further shaped and sanded. *Photos, courtesy artist*

STEAM BENDING

Construction of a steam chamber can be expensive or inexpensive depending upon the facilities, amount of steam to be generated, and the number of pieces to be steamed an hour. Basically, a steam chamber can be a teakettle on a stove with a hose to a wooden box; but that approach would take a long time. John Snidecor, California State University, Long Beach, received a grant to create this more complex chamber using an aluminum tank reclaimed from a Douglas aircraft salvage yard. It has two steam tubes from the boiler.

The water is placed in the lower chamber, which is heated by a gas burner. All parts are of aluminum, copper, or other nonferrous metals that won't rust, except the burner which is not in contact with the water.

The wood strips are suspended in a rack that slides in through the end of the steam chamber. Mr. Snidecor's experimentations have shown that too much pressure can thwart the bend. Up to a certain point of pressure and time, the amount of steam won't make any difference, so an elaborate chamber is unnecessary. Steam under pressure is extremely dangerous, so a pressure system is not advised.

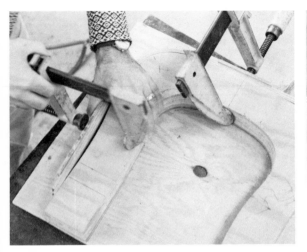

After steaming, the wood strips to be laminated are bent around the form and clamped until cool (about a half hour). The number of laminates involved depends on the thickness of the strips and the degree of the curve. If more than 5 or 6 layers are involved, he bends two series and then glues them together. But no glue is used in the first clamping.

As the clamps are tightened, you can see the space close between the strips and the form. An extra piece of scrap wood is placed alongside the laminated strips to hold the curve along a greater distance and to prevent the strips from being dented by the clamp.

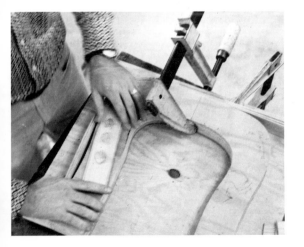

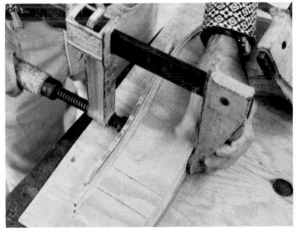

Extra blocks are also shaped to fit around the corner so the curve will be as even as possible.

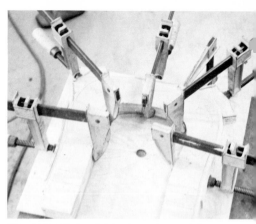

The strips are completely clamped around the form using the extra side and top curved blocks.

When the strips are unclamped they retain only about one half of the bend and tend to spring back. When the laminates are glued they will form a rigid configuration almost precisely the configuration of the form. This allows for multiple production of a number of identical curved forms not possible if the shape was to be solely steam bent from a thick piece of wood.

Now the bent pieces will be glued and reclamped. First rub a coat of wax along the edge of the form to act as a release agent.

Use a small paint roller to spread the glue onto the laminates.

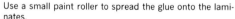

Be sure the surfaces are completely covered so that air pockets won't form between the laminated boards.

The glue covered strips are reclamped around the form. Use additional clamps on the ends to line up the top of the laminated strips with the top of the form.

The laminated steam bent strips are fashioned into a cradle, in progress, by John Snidecor. *Demonstration by John Snidecor, California State University, Long Beach*

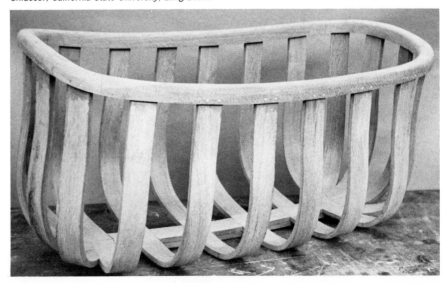

The following demonstration by William A. Keyser, School for American Craftsmen, Rochester Institute of Technology, Rochester, New York, illustrates another approach to steam bending. Mr. Keyser bends thick pieces of boards as opposed to laminating thin strips. The edges of the boards are chamfered to facilitate bending; they are held to the form with a bending strap that he has fashioned for the purpose and these can be seen in the photos.

The steam unit is a simply built wooden box with an opening at one end for sliding the wood in and out.

The steam is generated by a wall paper steamer connected to the box with hoses. Additional hoses carry away the condensation.

The curved form is attached to a post fitted with winches and chains.

Bending straps are ⅛-inch-thick steel with end fittings that will accept the hooks of the chains attached to winches. Straps help prevent the outer cells on the convex, stretched side, from expanding and consequently losing structural strength.

182

When the wood is pulled from the steam cabinet it is quickly placed against the form with a holding strap around it.

When bending a thick piece of stock, either air- or kiln-dried, the degree of the bend is limited. There is no scientific documentation on this type of bending procedure. Mr. Keyser's policy is always to bend two or three more pieces than he will actually need because of the tendency of the wood to crease and crack from the bending procedure. Sometimes he uses an additional drying jig to speed up the process. After bending the stock against the form for a short time, he clamps it to a form of the same shape so he can reuse the original bending form. He allows three to four days for drying before doing additional work; drying time depends upon the type and moisture content of the wood and the season.

The center is clamped first; the clamp is set into a hole at the base of the form.

The clamped and tightened wood has been fully pulled against the form.

A clamp is placed on each side of the center clamp, the chains are attached to the bending strap and the winches are tightened evenly on each side until the wood is pulled tightly against the form.

Detail shows the clamping at center and the hookup of the bending strap. *Demonstration: William A. Keyser*

William Keyser has fashioned a special form for bending legs used with specific furniture designs.

The wood stock, about two inches wide and eighteen inches long, is steamed and placed in the jig, and clamped.

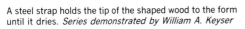

A steel strap holds the tip of the shaped wood to the form until it dries. *Series demonstrated by William A. Keyser*

For compound curves a form can be very complex. Bob Falwell, fashioned this form for creating the banisters used on the staircase, below.

A piece of straight wood stands vertically next to the curved, laminated strips that were made on the banister form.

Staircase (in progress). Bob Falwell.

CRADLE. Edward G. Livingston. 36 inches high, 43 inches wide, 24 inches deep. American black walnut. Laminated and bent members. *Courtesy, Sterling Associates, Palo Alto, Calif.*

SPRINGER #1. C. R. Johnson. 8 feet long. Walnut. Seat deflects from 22 to 18 inches off floor. The support is stack laminated, bent and bolted to the floor, the seat is edge laminated and carved.

ALTAR, LECTERN, CREDENCE TABLE, AND CROSS. William A. Keyser. Walnut. Steam bent with traditional joinery. (Interfaith Center, State University of New York at Geneseo.) *Photo, Donald L. Smith*

ELLIPTICAL SHELL DESK. Jere Osgood. Walnut.
Closed and open views. *Photos, Tom Millea*

cabinets, desks, doors

7

"Cabinet" is the term usually applied to describe pieces of furniture whose chief use is for storage. Peoples who had little need for seat furniture developed cabinets. Even in cultures such as that of the Japanese, in which few specialized furniture forms evolved, cabinet pieces are found.

A cabinet is essentially a frame with a movable panel. The simplest forms are boxes, and containers with a lid that opens to allow access. The lid may slide or be fastened with hinges, hasps, or catches. The six-sided box made by early peoples hasn't changed much. As in ancient times, boxes are still made from wood, metal, hide, clay, paper, and frequently covered and embellished with decoration.

Cabinets developed once the box was lifted off the floor and placed on legs. Such improvements as a drawer (essentially a box within a box), interior compartments, and fronts that dropped or opened sideways led to the development of specialized furniture forms such as the marriage coffer, the commode, the desk, the breakfront, and the variety of storage cabinets that have evolved through the centuries in different cultures.

The modern craftsman most often creates a sculptural cabinet form for his own use, or for a client's home or office. The supporting members, the drawers, doors, and handles, provide the opportunity for making a unique statement with the woods.

Milon Hutchinson's expressive approach to design is in the application of unusual detailing on the doors of a cabinet or desk more than in the shape itself.

Federico Armijo, Tom Bendon, Jere Osgood, and Robert Whitley explore the curvilinear potential of wood in their desk designs. Michael Bock's desk exhibits a classical simplicity but achieves the sculptural concept through the rounded edges of the interior compartments and handles that flow within the drawer fronts. The various solutions for legs and supporting members should be carefully observed.

HUTCH CABINET. Milon
Hutchinson. 7 feet high, 3 feet
wide, 20 inches deep. English
walnut. The incised geometric
designs are created with improvised bits made by the artist and used in a drill press
or overhead router. *Courtesy,
artist*

Above, left: Curved lines are made with the router.

Above, right: An improvised hand ground steel bit is used to make circles within the curves.

Milon Hutchinson also uses the shaped bits to make repeat circles next to one another as shown at right. The checked design at left was made with a router. *All photos, courtesy artist*

       William Keyser's interest in and attention to the use of curved members created by bending is emphasized especially in the ark with the barrel stave construction utilizing compound bends. John Cederquist explores the combination of wood with formed leather in his small wall hanging storage units.

       Sculptural doors are a logical outgrowth of cabinet furniture. Only a few craftsmen have developed significant statements in the artistry of modern doors, but it appears to be an area that is gaining wider appreciation. For the most part, such doors are made by the craftsman for himself. Slowly, homeowners, interior decorators, and architects are beginning to visualize the importance of the door as more than an entrance; it can set a mood that would greatly enhance a building. The door may be conceived along with the design of a building, then it is shaped, carved, and created to utilize harmonious materials as in the examples by Svetozar Radakovitch and Federico Armijo. Or the facade may be applied to an existing door, assemblage fashion, such as those made by Mabel Hutchinson.

       In every case, structural and weight problems, hardware and color, and weathering considerations must be major concerns of the designer.

Detail of cabinet suggests the various geometric designs one can achieve with the simple tools shown. Milon Hutchinson.

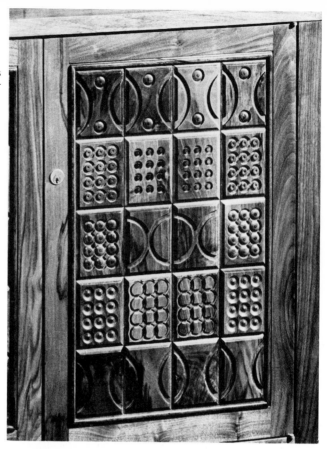

A series of "routed" blocks based on repeat squares and rectangles are mounted for an outdoor screen. Milon Hutchinson.

The lathe, usually used for turning spindles and bowl forms, has been adapted to circular designs within a square by Milon Hutchinson. The block of wood is mounted on the holding plate; the tool rest is adjusted so it faces the block and the cutting is done with the chisel. The radiating lines were first made on the router. Mr. Hutchinson proves the premise that one can adapt the tools to all kinds of statements when the imagination is fired.

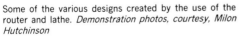

Some of the various designs created by the use of the router and lathe. *Demonstration photos, courtesy, Milon Hutchinson*

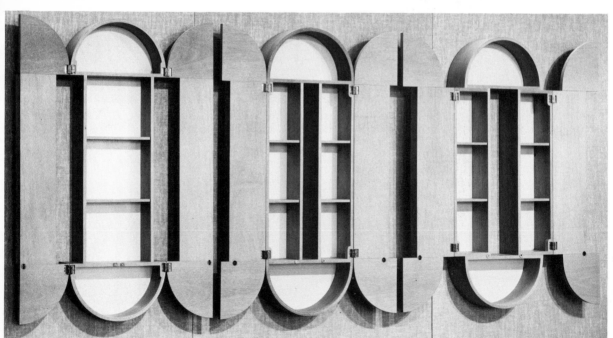

TRIPTYCH CABINETS. William A. Keyser. 48 inches high,
132 inches wide. Ramin wood using traditional construction techniques (closed and open views). *Photo, Donald L.
Smith*

ARK. William A. Keyser. 90 inches high, 72 inches wide, 36 inches deep. Teakwood. Steam-bent and barrel-staved construction (for open view see color section). *Photo, Donald L. Smith*

CABINET. William A. Keyser. 60 inches high, 56 inches wide, 15 inches deep. Walnut with zippered red vinyl doors. Steam-bent members and traditional joinery. *Photo, Donald L. Smith*

CABINET WITH FIVE LEGS. Bob Falwell. 51 inches high, 24 inches wide, 16 inches deep. Pennsylvania cherrywood.

Above, right: BAR. Roger Deatherage. 60 inches high, 18 inches wide, 17 inches deep. African mahogany. The two doors open in the center and reveal shelves for liquor and bar glassware.

Open view of Roger Deatherage's bar.

SHEET MUSIC CHEST. Bud Tullis. 48 inches high, 24 inches wide, 18 inches deep. Ten-drawer cabinet is completely walnut including the drawer interiors. *Courtesy, artist*

DRAWERS FOR JEWELRY. Terry A. Smith. 6 feet high. Padauk, rosewood, and metal. *Courtesy, artist*

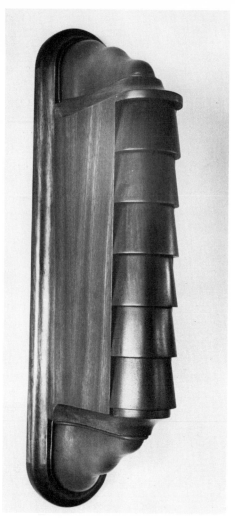

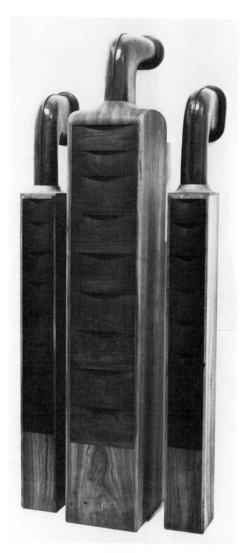

STORAGE CHESTS. John Cederquist. Three small hanging storage units utilize wood with formed and stitched leather curved members. *Courtesy, artist*

CHEST. Tom Tramel. 36 inches high, 22 inches wide, 16 inches deep. East Indian rosewood. The sculptural concept used for the handles is carried out on all side surfaces. *Photo, Tom Tramel*

JEWELRY CHEST. Maximiliano F. Chavez. 18 inches high, 16 inches wide, 14 inches deep. Walnut. Set on a swivel. Hand rubbed oil finish. *Courtesy, artist*

ROLLTOP DESK. Federico Armijo. 42 inches high, 7 feet long, 36 inches deep. Walnut. The swirling pattern of the supporting side members is echoed in the drawer fronts and knobs. *Courtesy, artist*

DROP LEAF DESK. Michael Bock. Supports for the leaf slide in and out at the sides. Cherry, walnut, and rosewood. *Photographed at the Richmond Art Center, Richmond, Calif.*

BONNIE'S DESK. Tom Bendon. 42 inches high, 22 inches wide. Rolltop; black walnut. Open and closed views. *Courtesy, artist*

WRITING DESK. Robert C. Whitley. American black walnut. Sculptured trestle base. Drawer fronts have been carved from a single 2-inch-thick board and a hand pull strip is worked into the carving. *Courtesy, artist*

CIRCULAR DESK. John Makepeace, F.S.I.A. Specially designed for a translator, the desk has adjustable shelving
for dictionaries, index systems, stationery, and recording
equipment. Sycamore finished with burnished lacquer,
acrylic, and other finishes. © *and courtesy, artist*

CORNER CABINET. John Bauer. 30 inches high. Oak and
Honduras mahogany. *Courtesy, Sterling Associates, Palo
Alto, Calif.*

WALL HUNG CHEST. Paul Sisko. 2 feet high, 6 feet wide, 14 inches deep. Walnut with stainless steel doors. *Courtesy, artist*

END TABLE SPEAKER CABINET. Paul Sisko. Teak and stainless steel. *Courtesy, artist*

Paul Sisko demonstrates the procedures for making a cabinet with stainless steel doors as shown on the preceding page. *Above:* After the basic parts of the cabinet are joined, glued, and clamped, the relief areas are carved out with a router.

Top right: The stainless steel doors are designed, shaped and welded.

Right: The welds are ground until the surface and joined areas are smoothed.

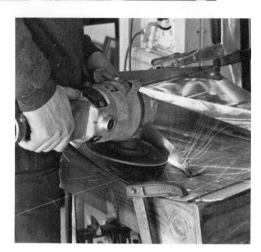

The doors are adjusted to fit the front of the cabinet. *Courtesy, artist*

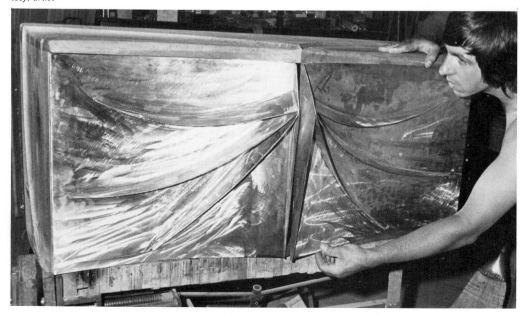

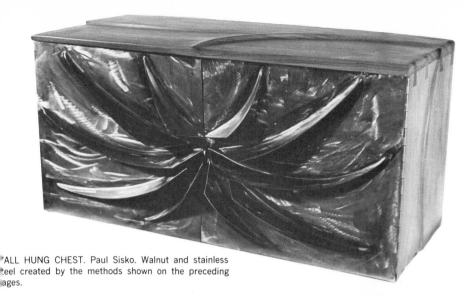

WALL HUNG CHEST. Paul Sisko. Walnut and stainless steel created by the methods shown on the preceding pages.

COMMUNION TABLE. Paul Sisko. Cherrywood and stainless steel.

COFFEE TABLE. Paul Sisko. 17 inches high, 32-inch-square top. Walnut base with stainless steel top.

OCCASIONAL TABLE. Paul Sisko. 17 inches high, 24-inch diameter. Welded aluminum base. The piece can be made with different wood tops in solid walnut, cherry, or teak or with a laminated walnut top as shown. *All photos, courtesy, Paul Sisko*

DOORS AS SCULPTURAL FURNITURE

Mabel Hutchinson carefully arranges geometrically shaped woods of assorted colors and types for a pair of doors in a private residence. After the scrap wood is shaped (most are left over from other projects) it is tumbled to smooth in the same way as stones are tumbled for lapidary work. *Courtesy, artist*

The unit for "tumbling" the wood is improvised using a basket turned by a belt attached to an old bicycle wheel with a motor attached. Scraps come from the cutoffs used in Milon Hutchinson's and Jocko Johnson's pieces.

DOORS. Mabel Hutchinson. Intricately balanced repetitive geometric shapes enhance the entranceway to the artist's home. *Courtesy, artist*

Two door designs for cabinets by John Kapel. *Above:*
Rosewood pieces are cut on a band saw and fitted as a door
on a wall-hung cabinet. *Right:* Sculpted and built up walnut
shapes emphasize a curvilinear composition and create
shadowing in the relief areas. It has the appearance of
windswept sand. *Photos, courtesy artist*

CARVED DOOR. Federico Armijo. 7 feet high, 3 feet wide, 3 inches deep. Oak, carved on one side. *Courtesy, artist*

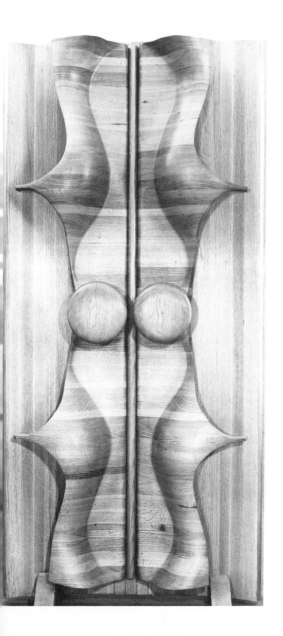

SCULPTURED DOUBLE DOOR UNIT. Maximiliano F. Chavez. The unit is 7 feet high, 3½ feet wide, 1¾ inches deep. Laminated red oak with turned door pulls. Hand-rubbed oil finish. *Courtesy, artist*

Sculptor Svetozar Radakovitch's wood doors are individually designed for the site. The subtle carving is often combined with surprises and unique details. Chunks of colored glass are set in to give light, color, and textural relief to the woods; the bronze hinges may be sand-cast or cast by the lost-wax process. Any mechanical joinery devices are covered with decorative butterfly joints in different colored wood, caps, or pegs. *Opposite:* Odd size opening for a door called for a narrow stationary portion combined with a normal width door.

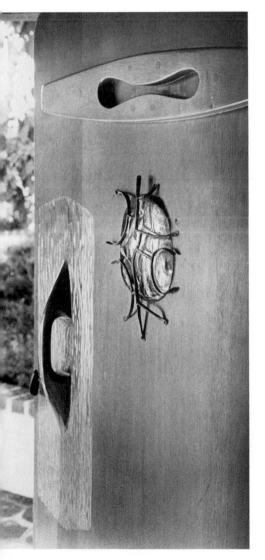

Above: The single door utilizes smooth and rough textured areas; the edge joining of the two boards is decoratively covered.

Left: Detail of door contains a jewellike piece of rock held to the door with a cast metal webbing.

211

TABLE. Tom Lacagnina. 24 inches high, 36 inches wide,
20 inches deep. *Photo, Linn Underhill*

fantasy furniture

8

From the beginning of time man has taken refuge in fantasy and he has often expressed his hopes and fears, anxieties and dreams in the furniture he has created. The use of fantastic forms was usually based on animal shapes in early Egyptian, Greek, and Roman furniture. In African and other primitive cultures the basis of the form may be religious and spiritual and combined with animalistic imagery.

The many fantastic forms used for the members of the furniture; feet, legs, arms, and the ornaments grafted on since Renaissance days, include winged sphinx, griffon, and chimera. They all serve as inspiration for contemporary craftsmen who are intrigued by the whims and capriciousness of the forms that can be expressed in furniture.

The inventiveness involved in the examples in this chapter is a testimonial to the imaginativeness of the artist and his ability to bring that image to a finished object. Such an object may be unexpected as furniture, yet quickly accepted for any number of reasons; as a revolt against mass production, as wild, unrestrained fancy, as something that refreshingly opposes the machine age esthetic.

The artist is concerned with traditional materials and craftsmanship, but his use of a wider variety of materials is interesting and obvious. Fine woods beautifully finished continue to play a strong role as in the examples by Julian Harr, Ann Malmlund, Dennis Morinaka, Tom Lacagnina, and Andrew Willner.

Thomas Simpson emphasizes an idea more through surface decoration than basic form; that idea often is approached with tongue in cheek. Some of his whimsically imaginative pieces are almost macabre and cynical in their conception; for instance, a chair with such an elongated wraparound arm that it would be impossible to be seated in it.

Joshua Hoffman's inspiration is an outright adaptation of African ideology and surface treatment based on an in-depth study of the wood sculpture of the peoples.

Concrete, papier-mâché, fibers, foams, furs, and fiberglass are used to create texture and tactile, sensual qualities. A surprising play of materials and ideas will be found in the glass tables by Dan Dailey.

213

General shaping of boards is accomplished with a radial
arm saw by Julian Harr and an assistant in Harr's Chicago
studio.

Right: A roughly carved laminated table leg.

Four pieces of board cut to outline shape of a table leg.
These will be glued and clamped, then carved.

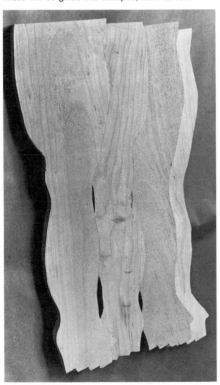

Egyptian folding camp bedstead of wood. Tomb of Tutankhamen, Thebes. The legs and feet show how early forms
were related to animals. It also illustrates the importance
of portability. *Courtesy, Griffith Institute, Ashmolean Museum, Oxford*

Another shaped leg, made of laminated and end glued
pieces, is being bolted to a horizontal member. The bolts
will be concealed under dowels where necessary.

CENTERPIECE TABLE. Julian Harr. 30 inches high, 44-inch diameter. Teak, ash, African mahogany, with cherry legs. A face is carved in the center and a glass jar is supported beneath the mouth to hold flowers. When the jar is filled it is as though the bouquet is coming from the mouth of the carved face.

Detail of center carving in table above.

Details that will be used in Julian Harr's furniture are carefully carved. Colored stones will be set into the eye sockets.

Chair arms as "arms" will become parts of the sculptural furniture forms.

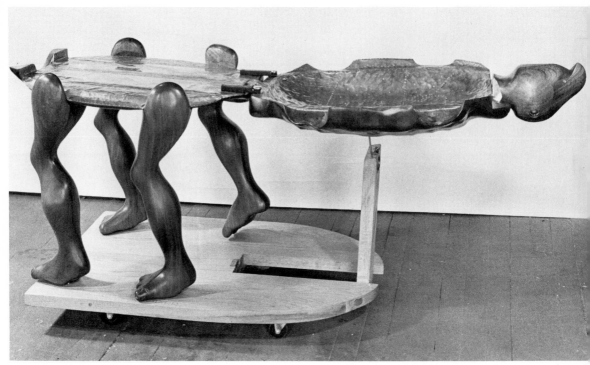

TURTLE SERVER. Julian Harr. Server is 30 inches high, open, 79 inches long. African teak, mahogany. Copper interior. The copper lining can be used as a serving adjunct to the wood table portion at the left.

Below: The table becomes pure sculpture when closed.

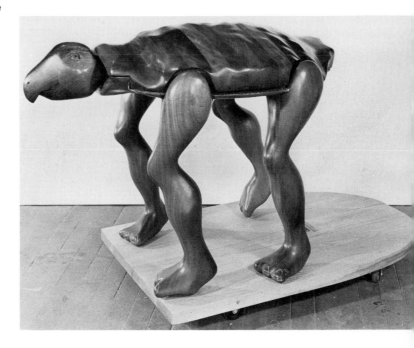

TABLE FOR SIX. Julian Harr. Table is 27 inches
high, 30 inches wide. Southern white pine with
table settings routed out to accommodate dish and
utensils. The overall shape is that of a cutting
board.

MRS. BOSCH. Julian Harr. Figure is 24 inches high, 6 feet
wide, 23 inches deep. Common pine laminated, and
shaped. The scales are incised. Glass top.

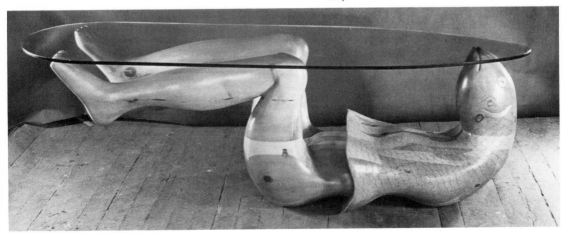

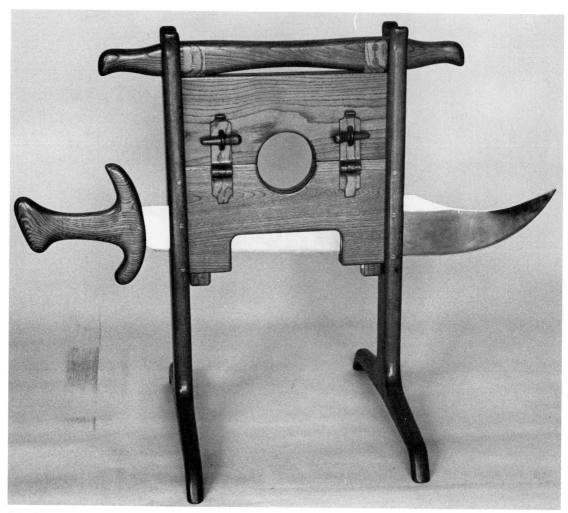

GUILLOTINE. John Gaughan. The guillotine is 3 feet high,
3 feet wide, 2 feet deep. Oak. Handcrafted for use by a
magician. The locks are wood and only the vicious blade
with its secret center break is metal.

CHEST OF DRAWERS. Dennis M. Morinaka. 5½ feet high,
37 inches wide, 29 inches deep. The interior superstruc-
ture to hold the drawers is oak; the laminated sides are
African Mansonia, drawn faces are carved into Brazilian
walnut drawer fronts: the drawer sides and bottoms
are black walnut, rosewood and aromatic cedar. *Courtesy,
artist*

Opposite: THE CLOTHES TREE. Candace Knapp. 6 feet high. Laminated redwood with drawers, doors, mirror, window, and branches from which to hang coats. *Courtesy, artist*

Left: CHAIR. Candace Knapp. 8 feet high, 28-inch diameter. Laminated pine. Interior has a painted sky with white fur clouds, upholstered mountains, foothills, lake and embroidered fish. Stars cut in the dome allow light to shine in. *Courtesy, artist*

Right: HAUNTED CABINET. Candace Knapp. 62 inches high, 17 inches wide, 8 inches deep. Laminated pine burnt and stained. There are three compartments. The top compartment is lined with copper to permit use of a small candle which allows the window eyes to glow. *Courtesy, artist*

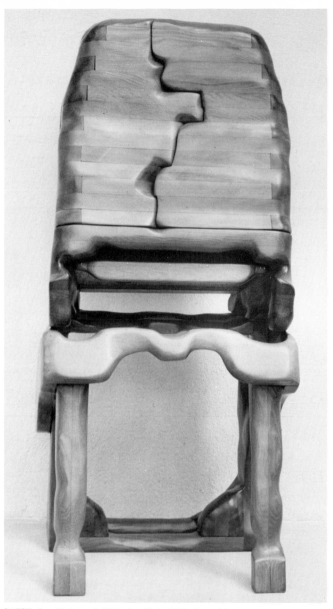

CHEST. Ann Malmlund. 55 inches high, 24 inches wide, 24 inches deep. Pine. Whimsically shaped legs support a cabinet with off-centered divisions within. *Photo, Tom Tramel*

Opposite: CHEST. Ann Malmlund. 6 feet high, 42 inches wide. Pine. Doors within doors open and shut to reveal various shaped compartments. *Photo, Tom Tramel*

224

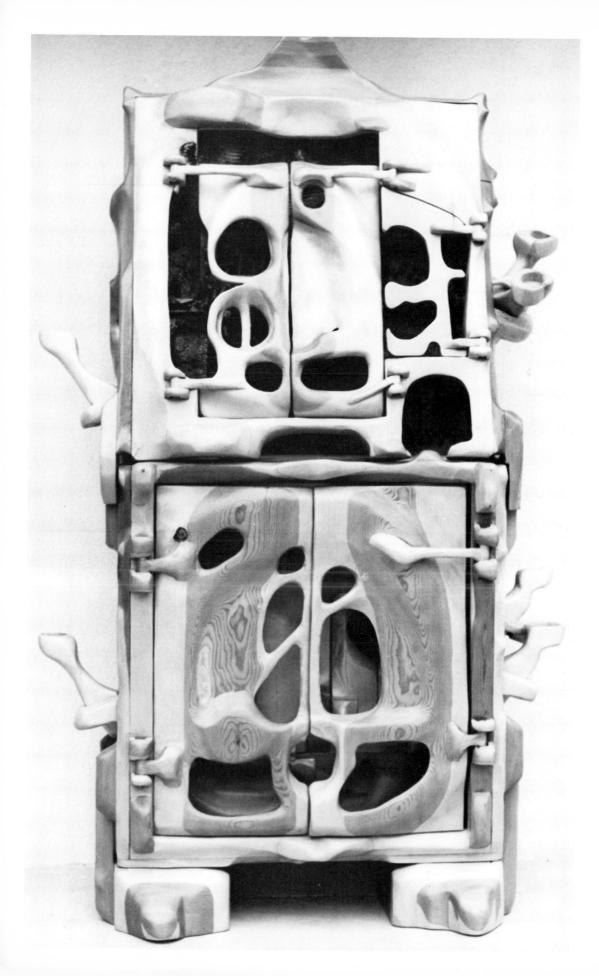

LADIES' CHAIR. Lilian A. Bell. Fabric, metal, paper, and plastic foam over a wood frame. *Photo, Tony Bell*

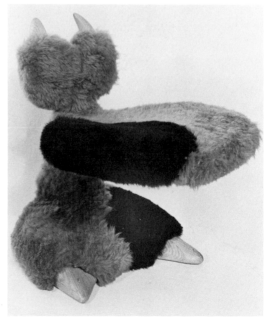

BENCH. Robert Falwell. 26 inches high, 20 inches wide, 22 inches deep. Red oak covered with blue and black fur, horns added.

FANTASY LAMP. Ann Malmlund. 54 inches high, 20 inches wide, 20 inches deep. Pine.

LAMP (in progress). Julian Harr. 75 inches high, approximately 67 inches wide. Laminated lamp is made completely from scraps of different woods culled from larger projects; mahogany, oak, ash, teak, rosewood, plywood, elm, and sugar pine.

DINING OR DESK CHAIR. John Bauer. Mahogany and walnut with ebony inlay. *Courtesy, artist*

Above, right: ARMCHAIR. John Bauer. Mixed woods; Japanese oak, cypress, Honduras mahogany, Mansonia. The diving pelican is inlaid. *Courtesy, artist*

CRADLE. Andrew Willner. 2½ feet high, 4½ feet wide, 2½ feet deep. Butternut and bubinga (African rosewood). *Courtesy, artist*

DRAGONFLY COFFEE TABLE. Andrew Willner. 15 inches high, 5 feet wide, 4½ feet deep (body of fly). Walnut and curly maple. *Courtesy, artist*

SERVING CART. Andrew Willner. 3 feet high, 5 feet wide, 2½ feet deep. Wormy chestnut and bubinga (African rosewood). *Courtesy, artist*

FIVE-SIDED PEDESTAL TABLE. John Bauer. Poplar, with inlay of walnut, cherry, teak, and mahogany. *Courtesy, artist*

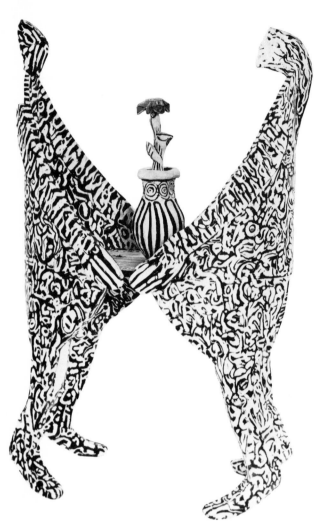

TWO PEOPLE CARRYING THEIR SEX AROUND. Thomas
Simpson. 5 feet high. Pine painted with black and white
acrylic. The table holds a flowerpot which contains a music
box. *Courtesy, artist*

"GYRAFF" GRANDFATHER'S CLOCK. Thomas Simpson. 7
feet high. Pine painted with black and white acrylic. *Courtesy, artist*

WALNUT CHAIR. Joshua Hoffman. Walnut.

WALNUT TABLE. Joshua Hoffman. Walnut. Mr. Hoffman's furniture designs are often based on images from African cultures. He spent much time photographing and studying the works and furnishings of the natives.

These pieces by Tom Lacagnina present a fluid sculptural approach to a variety of forms that have the basic ingredients of fantasy furniture combined with fine craftsmanship. *All photos, Linn Underhill*

Above: LAMINATED TABLE (open and closed views). Tom Lacagnina. 30 inches high, 24 inches wide, 24 inches deep.

TABLE WITH STACKED BASE. Tom Lacagnina. 18 inches high, 36 inches wide, 24 inches deep.

TRIPLE COCKTAIL TABLE. Tom Lacagnina. 20 inches high, 36 inches wide, 12 inches deep.

TABLE WITH HANDLE. Tom Lacagnina. 18 inches high, 18 inches wide, 18 inches deep.

TABLES. Bill Bayer. Created from assorted woods, old signs, and recycled materials, plus acrylic paint. Says Mr. Bayer: "My tables are the nifty result of working with tools and joining devices and arcane ideas."

Above: WASHINGTON'S BIRTHDAY. 17 inches high, top, 18 X 22 inches.

CAUTION TABLE WITH HEART. Bill Bayer. 15 inches high, top, 12 X 18 inch yellow road sign wood. TABLE WITH HOLE HEART. 13 inches high, top 15 X 15 inches, cedar legs, fir top, colored with color pencils and acrylics.

FLYING COCKTAIL TABLE. Bill Bayer. 23 inches high, 36 inches wide, 22 inches deep. *Photos, artist*

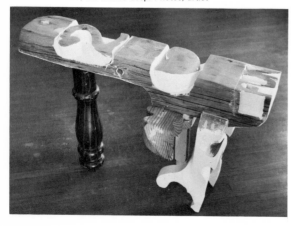

VANITY TABLE. Dan Dailey. 5 feet high. A glass and mirror table is a display and functional item for the eight glass perfume bottles made like rocket ships. *Courtesy, artist*

DOG TABLE. Dan Dailey. 21 inches high. Crystal glass. Fragile-looking blown glass with a plate glass surface. The artist transposes a small object to functional sculpture. *Courtesy, artist*

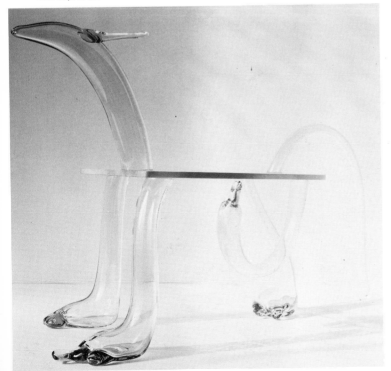

CHILDREN'S PLAY SCULPTURE. Pat Diska. Carved stone. Furniture for the outdoors. Photographed at the quarry. *Photo, artist*

Chair in reinforced concrete. By Charles Semser of *Bluebeard and Wife* (*opposite, top*) in reinforced concrete. The finished furniture was created in precolored polyester.

Polyester and fiber glass taken from an epoxy mold of the
cement prototype *(above)*. *Courtesy, artist*

STOOLS. James Danisch. Approximately 13 inches high.
Stoneware using coiled and wheel-thrown procedures.
Incised and sprayed textures and multiple firings. *Photo,
M. D. Seitelman*

ROCKING HORSE. Lawrence B. Hunter. 44 inches high, 64
inches wide, 26 inches deep. Oak base. The horse is a
wood inner structure covered with papier-mâché and then
finally with fiberglass.

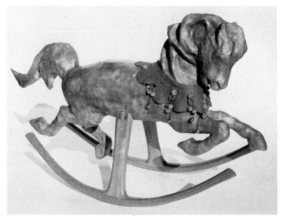

FANTASY BAR AND STOOL. Frank O. Gehry with his whimsical and intricate sculptural shapes created from cross-laminated layers of corrugated fiberboard. It can be used as a bar, desk unit, or reading table. *Photo, Pat Faure*

PAPIER-MÂCHÉ

Papier-mâché furniture can assume any number of whimsical shapes and decorations that give it an infinite potential. The process involves building an armature of wood, screening, and cardboard, or all three, and filling it out with whatever will yield the desired form; it might be newspapers as shown in the foundation for the photo *(below)* of the understructure of the Jaw chair by Mark Abrahamson, illustrated in the color section. The outer coat of fiberglass is durable and gives a finished appearance. A form can also be shaped over a simple wood armature with aluminum foil as in the People chairs by Connie von Hagen, page 243.

Papier-mâché is strong and durable; the finish depends on how well you have sealed the base materials and colored the work. Papier-mâché can be cut, sanded, assembled, and finished much as one works with wood. The paper layers are built up over the armature with small squares of torn heavy drawing or other papers and adhered with white glue. The paper is sealed with gesso. It can then be smoothed, painted, and decorated. The finish can be done with coats of plastic resin, acrylic varnish, or lacquer. For additional instructions and uses of papier-mâché for furniture, see *Papier-Mâché Artistry* by Dona Z. Meilach in the Crown Arts and Crafts series.

Armature for chair "Jaw" by Mark Abrahamson utilizes plywood, chicken wire, newspapers, and fiberglass. See finished chair.

Papier-mâché surfaces are created by applying squares of torn paper with white glue.

The surface has this appearance as the layers of paper are applied.

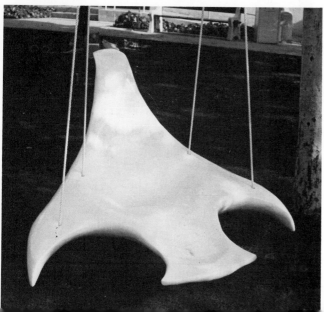

HANGING ROCKER. Gaylord Norcross. 6 feet wide, 7 feet long. After smoothing, sealing, and finishing with a fiberglass coat the papier-mâché rocker has a fool-the-eye appearance; it can be mistaken for all fiberglass or plastic. It offers an inexpensive creative concept for furniture design. *All photos, Larry Hunter*

KANGAROO ROCKER. Kenneth Langston. Papier-mâché painted with acrylics. The armature was carefully constructed of wood and shaped with screening; then stuffed with newspapers as the base for the layers of glued papers. The plywood armature must be carefully planned and may involve pattern drawings and a model built of balsa wood to determine the shapes needed and the balancing required. *Photos, Larry Hunter*

PEOPLE CHAIRS. Connie von Hagen. An existing wood chair was shaped out with crushed aluminum foil and then covered with papier-mâché and decorated. The polka dot "clothing" is a layer of paper tablecloth sprayed with a plastic finish. Face details are hand painted. *Courtesy, Alcoa*

leather, fur, fibers, and other media

9

Since furniture styles throughout history have overlapped and been handed down from one generation to the next, a study of strictly commercial furniture pieces and existing examples does not necessarily reflect the tastes and styles of an entire culture. Today, one can buy a style from any previous time period from showrooms that also show avant-garde modern designs. Still, all the furniture that is being designed is not necessarily in commercial showrooms. Archeologists two thousand years from now might be extremely puzzled if they turned up some of the one-of-a-kind craftsman-made pieces that do not reflect the general trends.

Many craftsmen who are expert with multiple craft media purposely, and sometimes accidentally or through necessity, apply these materials to furniture with marvelously original results. This chapter explores some of the mixed media and potpourri in furniture designs that incorporate fibers, leathers, furs, foams, vinyls, stoneware, and combinations of all of these with one another and with wood and plastic.

Mary Keepax of Canada is well known for stoneware wall pieces and sculptures; she has begun to use these pieces as a base for assorted small glass-topped tables. They have an undersea, organic appearance in the fragile-looking, white material. Libby Platus, an artist who works with fibers for large architectural commissions switched her thinking and experience to various other materials and techniques to create leather and fur swing-chairs.

Woven and knotted furniture pieces reflect the concern of the craftsmen's concept of having the furniture surround the user: to make him feel comfortable in a womblike setting that has a warmth and tactile quality.

Dan Wenger combines a metal frame with leather slings that become sculptural in their shaping within the frame. Federico Armijo combines his knowledge of woodworking with leather that is subtly shaped and sewn to coordinate and complement each other; it appears as organic and environmental as the desert-like California setting in which he works.

Stuffed fabrics, vinyls, and leathers are showing up in new ways; a completely different concept from the upholstered piece. These are an outgrowth of the soft

Opposite: CHAIR DESIGN. Federico Armijo. 50 inches high, 22 inches wide, 24 inches deep. Chestnut and oak with leather seat and back. *Courtesy, artist*

beanbag chair and inflatable items that became a commercial success a few years ago. The artists are exploring further the possibility of soft, low seating that can be rearranged in predictable and unpredictable ways.

The inspiration for some of the forms is obvious. They should make the beginner, as well as the experienced designer, realize that ideas for furniture design are the same as those that inspire every other art form. They can be organic as in Joyce Shettle-Neuber's "Cabbage Chair" and the lip-shaped seat titled "Marilyn." They can have man-made design origins as in the couch shaped like a baseball mitt and titled "Joe."

The examples on the following pages are by Dan Wenger of California. He utilizes simple, sturdy frames of steel painted flat black, burnished to a high luster and coated with polyurethane. The slings may be cowhide, red latigo, or suede laminated to both sides of 12-ounce red latigo, and more than one sling can be made so they are changeable. The steel gives a springiness to the design and the leather sling permits a gentle rhythmic motion and a shape that conforms to the user's body.

Right: DINING CHAIR. Dan Wenger.

Below: STOOL. Dan Wenger. 25 inches high. Latigo on steel frame.

Opposite, top: THE LOTUS CHAIR. Dan Wenger. 46 inches high. Suede laminated to both sides of red latigo.

Opposite, bottom: THE SOQUEL RECLINER so named for Soquel, Calif., home of the artist. Dan Wenger. 41 inches high, 53 inches long. *Photos, courtesy artist*

Above: TABLE AND CHAIRS. John Makepeace. Padded and wrapped with leather. © *John Makepeace. Photo, Sam Sawdon*

Left: TABLE. Mary Keepax. Glass top on a white stoneware and porcelain table base. *Credit: World Craft Council Conference, 1974 Canadian Selection*

Opposite, top: THE LOVE SEAT. Dan Wenger. 33 inches high. *Courtesy, artist*

Opposite, bottom: CHAIR. Ed Stiles. Walnut and leather. *Courtesy, Pasadena Art Museum, Pasadena, Calif. Photo, Richard Gross*

SWING. Libby Platus. Leather, fur, and cowhide over a steel frame. Leather strips have been pulled through the canvas backing with a latchet hook used in rugmaking; the canvas is then attached to the chair. *Photo, Phil Shuper*

SWING-LOUNGE. Libby Platus. 3 feet high, 6 feet wide, 3 feet deep. Leather, wool, fur, and cowhide. The demonstration on the following pages illustrates the development of the piece. *Photo, Phil Shuper*

Libby Platus describes the general procedure for creating
a swing, or other pieces of furniture, using a metal armature, rubber upholsterer's webbing, foam with leather, and
latchet hooked upholstery. *Photo series, David Platus*

Design and draw the swing shape. Make a
wire scale model of the armature with #20
annealed wire.

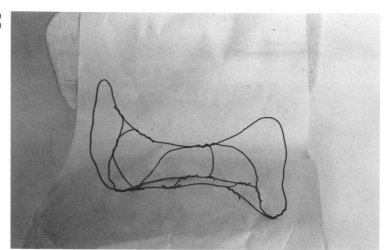

Work up an *actual size model* of the armature using a flexible, but sturdy, aluminum
wire. Hang the actual model from beams to
check on how it will hang, move, balance, etc.
Mark the places on the armature where holes
for attaching the chair will be.

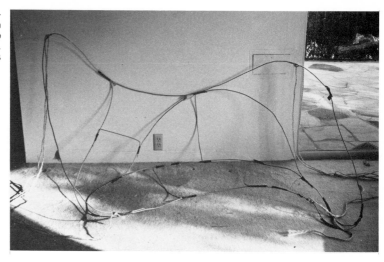

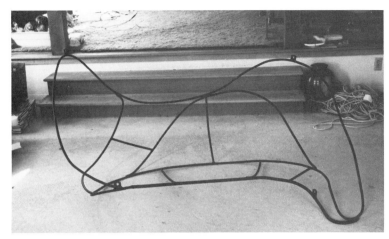

Make, or have made in a machine shop, the finished steel armature based on your aluminum wire model.

Sew rubber upholstery webbing to the steel armature using C-clamps to hold the webbing tight as you sew. To facilitate sewing, punch holes in the webbing with a leather punch.

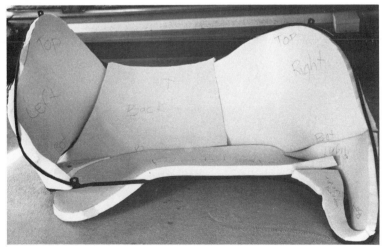

Make patterns for the foam stuffing and exterior leather upholstery. Cut and sculpt the foam to shape using an electric carving knife for the thick foam. To finish with upholstery, cover the foam with thin muslin. Cut a paper pattern and trace onto leather allowing 1-inch seam all around. Punch stitch holes in leather and sew pieces together using waxed linen in a curved upholstery needle.

Latchet hooked areas are made on separate shapes of rug canvas and then sewn to the leather.

WOVEN CHAIR ENVIRONMENT. Cindy Blake. 6 feet high, approximately 50-inch diameter. Natural dyed jute and cotton. *Courtesy, artist*

Opposite: HANGING CHAIRS. Gwynne Lott. Jute and linen woven over a ¼ inch steel frame in the bottom and very top.

Left: VICTORIA'S TOMBOY SISTER. *Collection Dr. and Mrs. Edward Rynes*

Right: WHITE SWING. *Photos, courtesy, artist*

Bottom: HAMMOCK. Gwynne Lott. 9 feet wide, 64 inches deep. Rayon tire belting woven in a loom-controlled lace weave. *Courtesy, artist*

KATARI. Gwynne Lott. Twined and braided dyed jute upholstery cord suspended with steel rings. All handwork was accomplished off the loom. *Courtesy, artist*

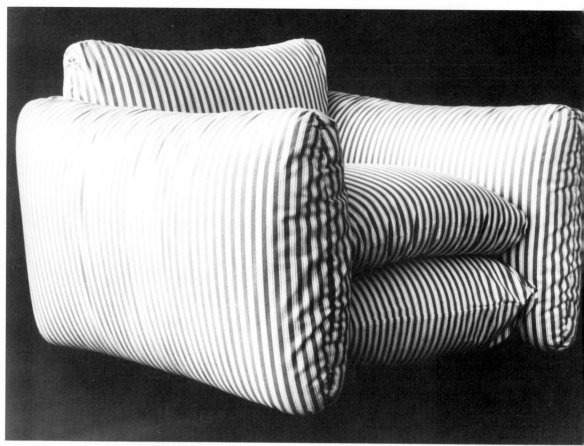

PILLOW ARMCHAIR. Phyllis Epstein. Modular steel spring
construction, urethane and Dacron covering, mattress
ticking upholstery (Fortress Inc., Los Angeles). *Courtesy,
La Jolla Museum of Contemporary Art, La Jolla, Calif.*

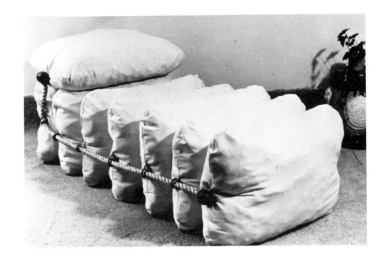

MULTIPLE SEATING UNIT. Vladimir Selepouchin. Polypropylene ropes strung through metal rings with wooden balls securing the ends enclose a series of cushions filled with polyurethane foam. The shape can be changed in multiple ways (Craft Associates). *Courtesy, Sachs, New York (design competition)*

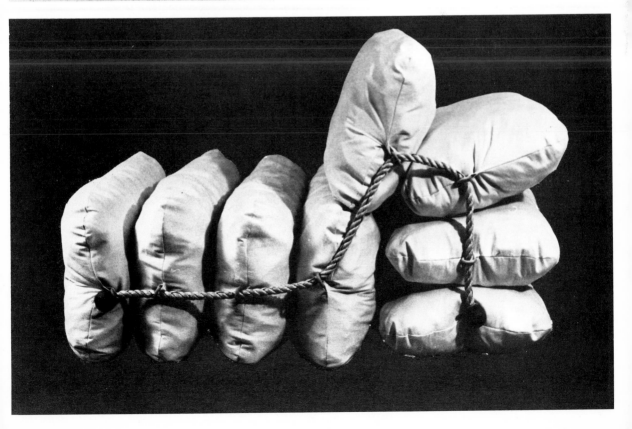

ZEN ZAFU CUSHIONS. Jeannie Campbell. Children's size, 5 inches high, 9-inch diameter; adult, 7 inches high, 13-inch diameter. Zippered fabric cover with Kapok stuffed form. Handles for carrying. *Photo, J. Patrick Stevens for Alaya Stitchery*

BESTIARY CUBE. Joyce Stack. 16-inch cube. Batik on cotton over a plexiglas cube with light inside. *Courtesy, artist*

CABBAGE. Joyce Shettle-Neuber. Foam base with stitched and quilted fabrics. *Photo, Larry Hunter*

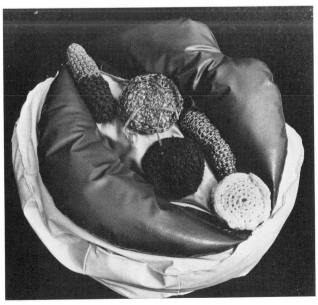

POP-A-PILL. Sherry H. Ball. Hassock with beanbag toss game. Hassock is vinyl and satin with foam filling; pills are crocheted with varied fillings. *Photo, J. Berman*

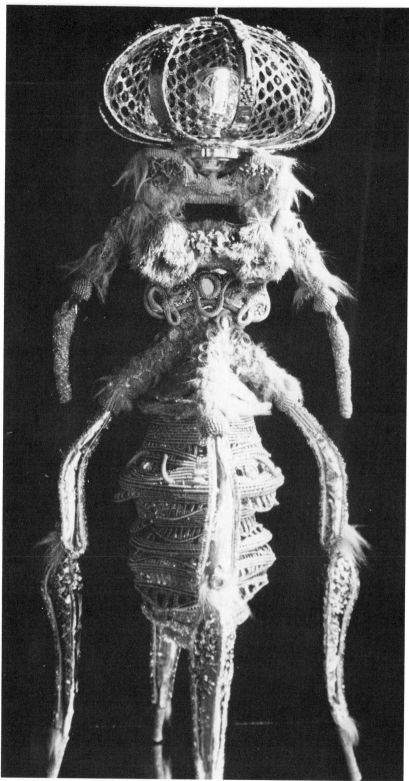

ILLUMINATED MUTATION. Stephen Thurston. 60 inches high, 26-inch diameter. Floor lamp using a variety of different kinds of silver materials: yarns, chrome strips, Mylar fabric, imitation fur, nickel-plated leather studs, chrome lamp fixtures, etc. Techniques are loom-woven tapestry and rya, frame loom-woven bands, crochet, stitchery, and macramé. *Courtesy, artist*

THE SENSUOUS CHAIR. Norma Minkowitz (*two views*). 32 inches high, 65 inches wide, 54 inches deep. Fibers and fabrics as stuffed and hanging forms. Sewing stitchery, crochet, and hooking. *Courtesy, artist*

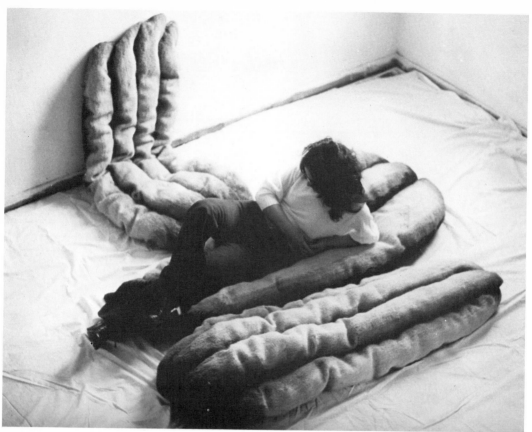

PROVISORIUM. Ritzi and Peter Jacobi. Woven stuffed
forms can be improvised to accommodate various shapes
and angles for versatile furnishings. *Courtesy, artists*

SULLIVAN. Shirley Saito. 24 inches high, 32 inches
square. Crochet over Styrofoam shape (*two views*).

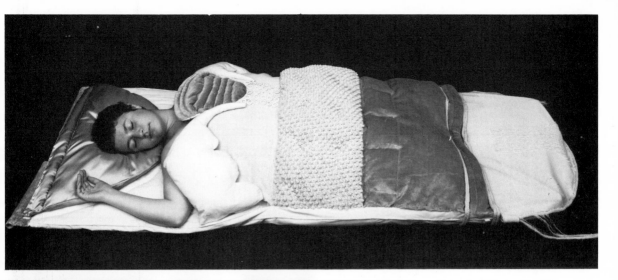

PORTABLE WORLD. Norma Minkowitz. 80 inches long, 33 inches wide. Sleeping bag or wall hanging of muslin, satin, velvet and Dacron using knitting, trapunto, crochet, hooking and padding. *Photo, Little Bobby Hanson*

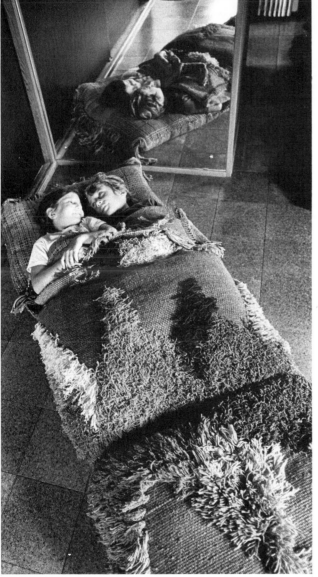

SLEEPING UNIT. Pat Swenson. Woven wool and synthetic fibers constructed on the loom. Rya knotting on the outside gives a tactile decorative addition. The piece can be placed on the floor or set on a frame to become a couch. *Courtesy, artist*

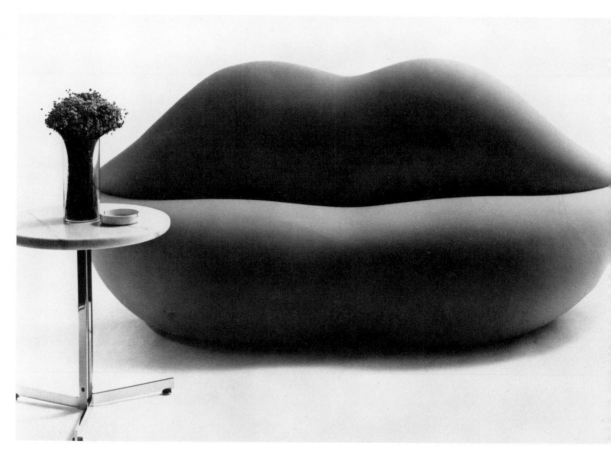

MARILYN. Studio 65. 33 inches high, 81 inches wide, 34½ inches deep. Urethane foam covered with stretch nylon fabric (Stendig Inc., N.Y.). *Courtesy, La Jolla Museum of Contemporary Art, La Jolla, Calif.*

JOE—FIELDER'S MITT. DePas, D'Urbino and Lomazzi. 34 inches high, 65 inches wide, 42 inches deep. Foam upholstered in natural Italian leather. Two-seat sofa on casters. *Courtesy, Stendig Inc., New York*

DESK. John Makepeace. Sycamore and Lebanon cedar are combined with buffalo suede and hide with the hair on it. *© and courtesy, artist*

10

plastics

Painters, sculptors, and craftsmen have applied plastics to almost every expressive outlet ever since they took over the materials from the earliest industrial sources. This extremely versatile durable family of man-made materials was rapidly adapted to furniture that could be readily reproduced commercially. It is reasonable that the artist-sculptor-designer who turns his attention to furniture will also explore the possibilities offered him by plastics. Some of the pieces are one of a kind, others have been cast so that editions of the pieces can be made. They retain their high design ethic and sculptural context and may serve as stimulants for further investigation into the possibilities of plastics for furniture.

Plastic is a generic term for an assortment of by-products of what we use as fuel: carbon-containing substances such as coal and petroleum, along with air, water, limestone, salt, sulfur, and other materials. The processes through which these substances go to result in plastics is complex and may be found in industrial and chemical books dealing with the plastics. For the purpose of this discussion, the different products normally used by furniture manufacturers are acrylics, polyester resins, epoxies, fiberglass and foams.

WHITE BRIDE. Altina Carey. Cast polyester and fiberglass with silk screen design applied. From a series of "Chairacters." *Collection, Clare Boothe Luce, Hawaii. Photo, courtesy, artist*

ACRYLICS are thermoplastic, which means the material can be heated and formed, reheated and re-formed. They are available in sheets, blocks, rods, tubes, and domes. Generally, these forms are manufactured by injection molding, extrusion, or casting processes. From these forms, artists can create flat, curved, and solid furniture shapes often combining a flat sheet of acrylic as a tabletop with tubes or rods for legs.

Acrylic can be treated much like wood; it can be sawed, drilled, glued, and polished in addition to its primary advantage of heating and shaping. It can also be vacuum-formed. Acrylic sheet is available in clear, transparent, opaque, and fluorescent coloring; a recent development is the mirror finish. Acrylic, when used for furniture, offers clarity and diffraction characteristics accompanied by its light weight and durability compared to glass. When glass is more than six inches thick, an object can barely be seen through it; but a thick slab of acrylic is clear and lightweight, thus affording unusual practical applications to furniture.

POLYESTER RESIN is one of the most useful materials for the designer because of its versatility and the many variations that can be incorporated into the materials. Starting as a pourable liquid the consistency of syrup, polyester resin can be cast, laminated, embedded, and carved. Forms are made by pouring the resin (it hardens with the addition of a catalyst) into a flexible or solid mold. Furniture designers can create an original, pull a mold from it, and re-create the design in any number of editions with a variety of texture and color variations if desired.

Some of the following characteristics of polyesters should be studied and experimented with before applying them to furniture designs. It is a fact that polyester resins are less expensive than acrylics, but some do not stand sunlight as well as acrylics. Polyesters can be rigid or flexible depending upon the formula used; they can be reinforced and impregnated with other materials for structural strength and to reduce shrinkage. The cure time for the polyesters can be controlled when necessary. Some polyesters can be fire retardant or resistant. A variety of fillers can be used to alter the transparency and color of the medium.

POLYURETHANES are versatile durable materials that have a range of characteristics and are used for coatings and paints, foams, both solid and flexible, rubberlike solids and adhesives. For furniture, the flexible urethane foams predominate. They are produced in gigantic, continuous blocks and slabs which are then cut into standard sizes and shapes. They are made in a closed mold and, using metering machines, they can be directly formed in various densities and colors. Heavier density foams have a smaller, closer cell structure labeled as 2.25 ± 0.15, while lighter density foams that have more air and are softer are labeled 1.15 ± 0.05 density.

Cutting flexible foam to shape is done professionally on a vertical band saw using a 1.1 hp motor but an electric carving knife or ordinary band saw used for cutting wood does a good job. A hot wire cutter may be used as well. Urethane foams may be adhered with epoxies and polyvinyl acetate; coloring should be done with water- or latex-based formula paints. Always experiment with the coating to be used to be sure an unknown element will not cause the foam to disintegrate.

When urethane foams are used for seating units, they are usually covered with fabric.

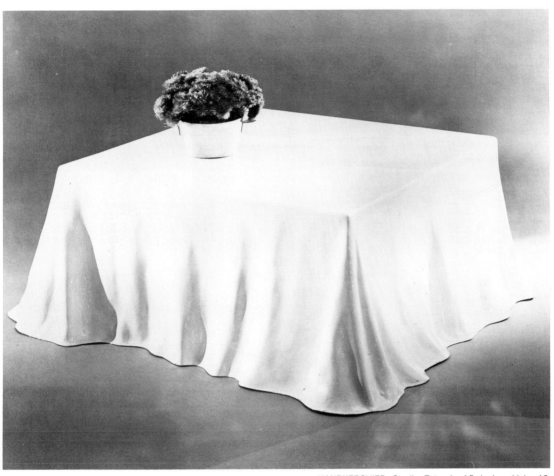

HANDKERCHIEF. Studio Tetrach. 15 inches high, 43 inches square. Coffee table made of polyester reinforced with fiberglass (Stendig Inc., New York). *Courtesy, La Jolla Museum of Contemporary Art, La Jolla, Calif.*

EGG WINE RACK. Donald Lloyd McKinley. 48 inches high.
Constructed of 4-inch diameter PVC (polyvinyl chloride),
a plastic pipe tubing. *Photo, artist*

Carla McCartin created the throne chair on page 273 from cut pieces and joints of ABS (acrylonitrile-butadiene-styrene) 1½-inch diameter plastic plumbing fixtures. Lawrence Hunter demonstrates the procedure. The materials are readily available and minimal; necessary pipe lengths for the design, different shaped couplings in 30°, 45°, and 160° bends and T joints, hacksaw, sandpaper, fine steel wool and Fuseon #945 or other plastic pipe cement. Pipe diameters are available up to 4 inches; they may be painted, if desired, with a compatible compound paint such as acrylics. *Demonstration by Lawrence B. Hunter*

Measure and cut the tube with a hacksaw, allowing a sufficient portion to fit within the joint.

Sand the burrs off the ends with about a #1 sandpaper.

Glue sets rapidly so you must work fast; daub glue on the inside.

Daub glue on the outer edge of the tube.

Insert length into joint and turn about one-fourth turn. If glue oozes, wipe off immediately as it is difficult to clean once it has dried.

Remove lettering carefully with a fine steel wool. The steel wool will take off the shiny surface so you can continue the scraping in portions to yield a combination of shiny and mat surface. The tubing may be painted or sprayed with a varnish finish.

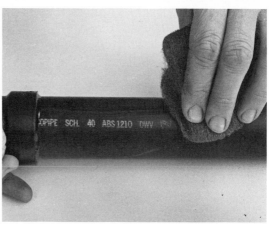

THRONE. Carla McCartin. The finished chair has been up-holstered with vinyl using some lightly stuffed areas. It could also be finished with fabric or leather.

Below: Detail of the joints using the 30° and 45° bends. *At right,* the back, arms, and legs are joined with T units.

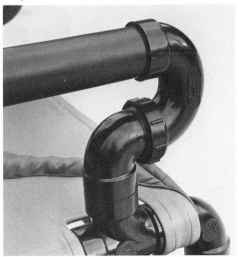

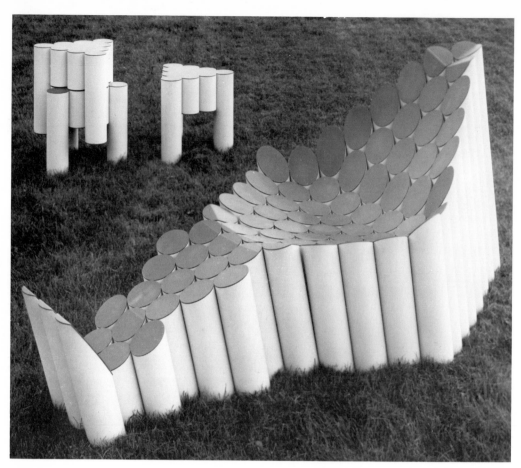

CHAIR AND OTTOMAN. Donald Lloyd McKinley. 78 inches long, 34 inches wide. Made with 4-inch-diameter PVC tubing with gray PVC caps. At rear is a combination stool/table that can be attached. 16 inches high. *Collection, Objects: USA Photo, artist*

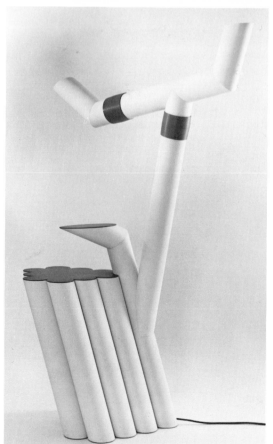

SWIVELING DOUBLE LAMP WITH CLUSTERED BASE. Donald Lloyd McKinley. 4-inch-diameter PVC tubing with gray caps. *Photo, artist*

TABLE. Charles Hollis Jones. Repeat cubes of acrylic sheet with stainless steel banding.

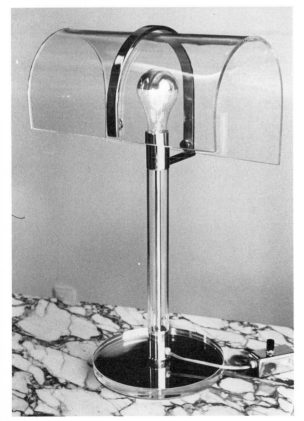

MAILBOX LAMP. Charles Hollis Jones. Acrylic sheet shaped over a wooden jig and used with an acrylic tube and base. Some stainless steel. Silver-topped Edison lightbulb is compatible with the sleek, modern design created by a master designer.

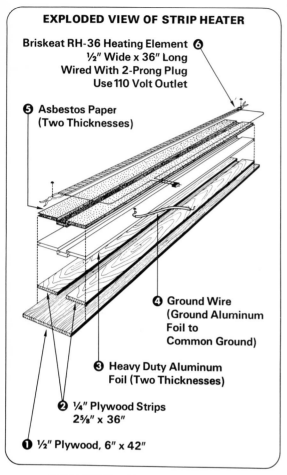

EXPLODED VIEW OF STRIP HEATER

Briskeat RH-36 Heating Element ❻
½" Wide x 36" Long
Wired With 2-Prong Plug
Use 110 Volt Outlet

❺ **Asbestos Paper**
(Two Thicknesses)

❹ **Ground Wire**
(Ground Aluminum
Foil to
Common Ground)

❸ **Heavy Duty Aluminum**
Foil (Two Thicknesses)

❷ ¼" **Plywood Strips**
2⅝" x 36"

❶ ½" **Plywood, 6" x 42"**

STRIP HEATER and its construction. This is a single element unit. Heaters can be improvised for a variety of types and sizes of bends.

HEATING AND SHAPING ACRYLIC SHEET

Acrylic sheet once heated can be given a variety of shapes. For straight bends a strip heater is used with one or more elements. For curves, an oven may be used and the sheet is shaped quickly over a jig which is usually made of wood. The procedure is very similar to bending wood in that the plastic is carefully held against the jig by another piece of wood or clamps provided they don't damage the surface of the acrylic while it is still soft. Small pieces of acrylic sheet can be heated and formed in a home oven; large pieces require larger ovens which may be created for the purpose or improvised from commercial baking ovens, used for pizzas and pies.

The single element strip heater shown above, and the double element made by William Fejer (*right*) can be easily copied, revised, and adapted.

The single element heater shown above costs about ten dollars to make. A special heating element manufactured by Brisco Mfg. Co. (Briskeat RH 36) is mounted to form a narrow heating surface that allows you to melt only portions of the acrylic plastic for spot shaping. To make the heater:

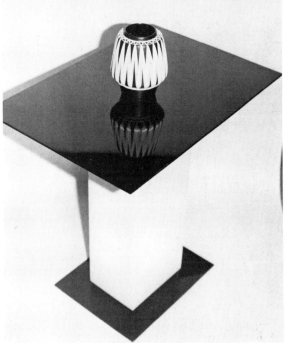

GAME TABLE. Frank Plaminek. ¾-inch acrylic sheet top and legs. Checkerboard has been silk-screened to bottom of tabletop. *Courtesy, Loop Acrylics, Chicago*

END TABLE. Frank Plaminek. Dark gray and white acrylic sheets are combined. *Courtesy, Loop Acrylics, Chicago*

STACKING CUBES. William Fejer. Rounded U shapes are combined for square and rectangular combinations that offer infinite variety. All bends were made on the simple double-strip heater. *Courtesy, Live From Chicago*

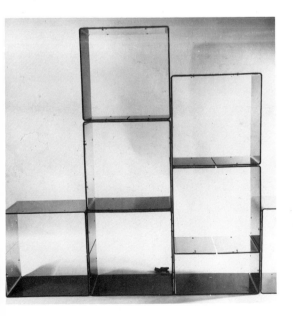

Acrylic sheet furniture designed by William Fejer takes
advantage of simple bends and curves and the use of
different sizes and colors of the material. In their simplicity, they retain a sculptural quality that has its foundation
in the designer's architectural background. *All photos,
courtesy artist*

Above: CHAISE. William Fejer.

Right: BAR. William Fejer.

Opposite, top: ROCKING LOUNGE. William Fejer.

Opposite, bottom: LOVE SEAT. William Fejer.

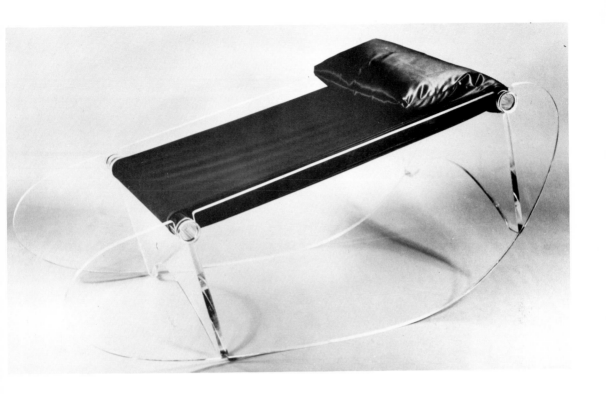

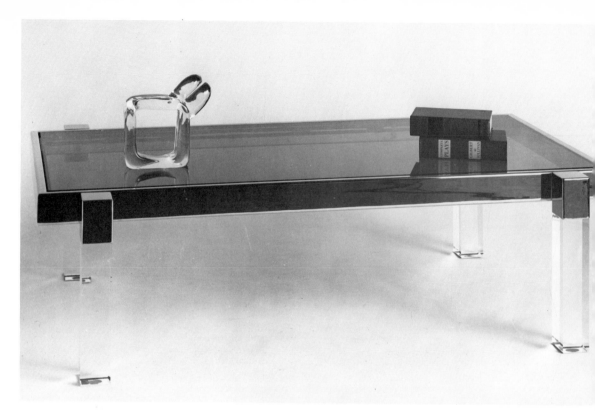

Charles Hollis Jones designs one-of-a-kind pieces that eventually are duplicated and/or slightly redesigned for special customers. He is especially interested in the sleek interplay of chrome or gold with clear or smoked plastics. All joinings are beautifully articulated so no screws, glue lines, or other mechanical joinings are evident. He is literally a virtuoso in the application of plastic sheet to contemporary furniture design.

COCKTAIL TABLE. *Charles Hollis Jones.*

BACKGAMMON TABLE WITH FLOOR MODEL MAILBOX STYLE LAMP. *Charles Hollis Jones.*

BOUDOIR CHAIR. Charles Hollis Jones. The flat pattern for chair base appears like this when flat. When the cut sheet is melted and placed over a wood jig, it assumes the form used at left. The rod is also shaped around a jig. The principle is essentially the same as steam bending wood.

Joints frequently found in the furniture by Charles Hollis Jones utilize stainless steel couplings specially designed and fabricated for the individual piece.

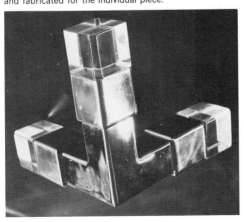

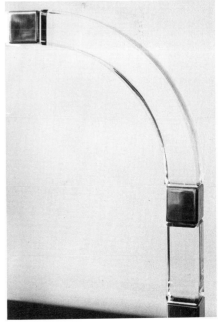

CHAIR. Frank Cummings. 31 inches high, 25 inches wide, 22 inches deep. The hand-carved oak original has been used as the model for the fiberglass chair, right. The artist made plaster piece molds which were used for casting the chair.

FOOTSTOOLS or SEATS. Ralph Massey. 14 inches high, 11-inch diameter. Polyester resin and acrylic. The original forms were made in papier-mâché. After a mold was pulled, the pieces were cast in polyester resin and painted with acrylics. *Collection, Mr. and Mrs. Stanley Scheinbaurm, Santa Barbara, Calif.*

OVAL DINING TABLE. Wendell Castle. 29 inches high, 48 inches wide, 56 inches deep. Cast polyester with fiberglass reinforcement. Castle's flowing, organic forms, originally interpreted in wood, have been developed in plastics. *Courtesy, artist*

MOLAR ARMCHAIRS. Wendell Castle. 26 inches high, 37 inches wide, 32 inches deep. Cast polyester with fiberglass reinforcement. The molded pieces are available with and without upholstery. Based on the organic dental form, the curves and voluptuousness are perfectly suited to the material that is fluid to start with. Although it hardens, it retains a fluidity in the design and in the resulting shadows. *Courtesy, artist*

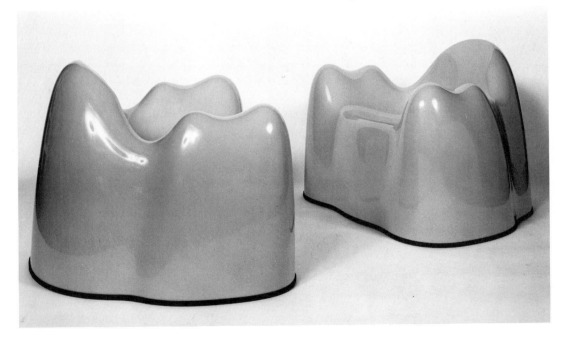

L'HOMME (THE MAN). Ruth Francken. The procedure used to create this unique chair is supervised by the artist. A limited edition of the chair in various colored plastic materials was sponsored by Scte. Eric and Xiane Germain, Paris. The base is made of stainless steel tubing. *Photos, Jack Nisberg*

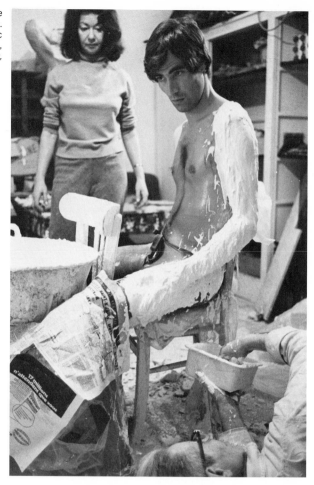

Plaster cast is made directly on a model.

The cast, smoothed and finished, is propped so that the base can be determined.

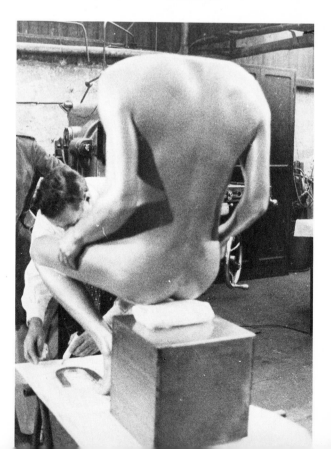

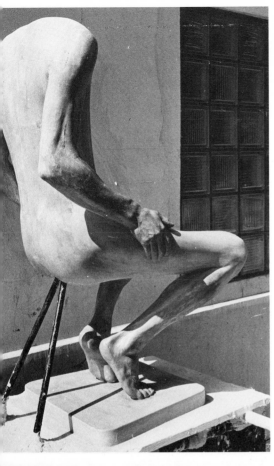
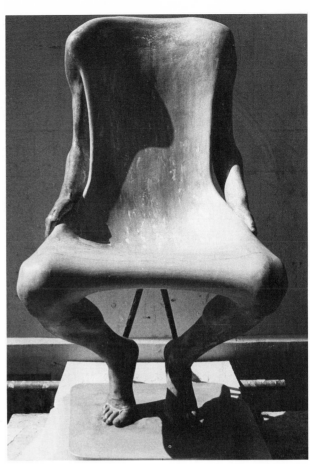

Plaster model, rear and front views.

CHAIR: L'HOMME in polyester with
stainless steel base.

Altina Carey's CHAIRACTER furniture in cast polyester and fiberglass was a natural evolution, she says, from a simple expedient chair design she made of wood and used as a canvas for whimsical drawings. They drew so much attention that she sought to refine the form, smooth it out, evolve it into a rich design. The early designs were used for stage settings in a theatrical performance and then they grew. *Photos, courtesy artist*

Above: CHAIRACTERS set around the den and pool of the artist's home.

Opposite, top, left: A plaster piece mold for the resin chairs.

Top, right: The artist in her studio and with a painted casting of the Cleopatra chair.

Bottom, left: THE LOVER BENCH. Altina Carey. 48 inches high, 22 inches wide, 38 inches deep. *Collection, Clare Boothe Luce, Hawaii*

Bottom, right: THE MEXICAN WEDDING. Altina Carey. *Collection, Albert Wohlstetter, Hollywood, Calif.*

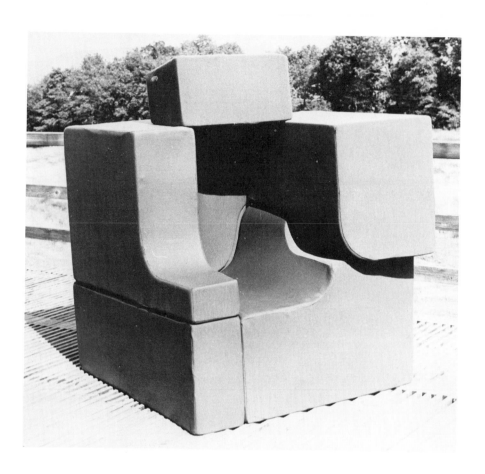

PARSONS CUBE. Robert J. Olsen. A seven-part polyurethane foam design incorporating basic furniture needs.
Pieces may be disassembled and used as separate seats,
bench, and stool forms. They can be readily stacked in
different arrangements to allow for sleeping, lounging, sitting. The four-foot cube weighs only 102 pounds. *Courtesy, artist*

WEDGE. Piero de Rossi. 34¾ inches high, 35½ inches wide, 35½ inches deep. Seat height can be varied depending on person's weight. Urethane foam upholstered in stretch nylon fabric. *Courtesy, Stendig Inc., New York*

DRUM LOUNGE CHAIR. Giuseppe Raimondi. 34½ inches high, 34½-inch diameter. Urethane foam body with easy-to-clean stretch fabrics. The slightly concave center becomes the seat, which adjusts naturally to the person's weight. *Courtesy, Stendig Inc., New York*

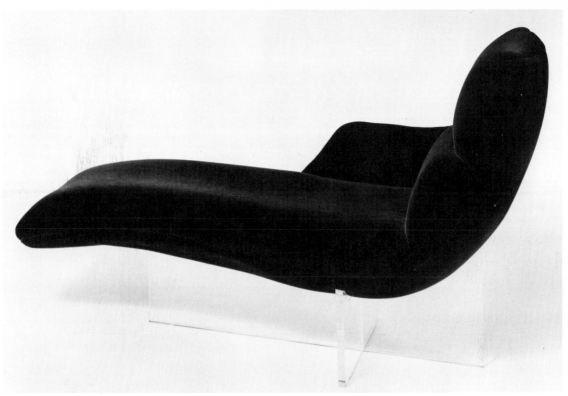

CHAISE. Sculptured form is polyurethane with velvet or other fabric nestled on a lucite base. *Courtesy, Vladimir Kagan Inc., New York*

LOUNGE. Geraldine Ann Snyder. Large piece, 20 inches high, 42 inches long, 16 inches wide. Small piece, 18 inches high, 6 inches wide, 18 inches deep. Stitched fabric packed with shredded foam. *Courtesy, artist*

SASSI (MOON ROCKS). Piero Gilardi. Set of three seats made of colored polyurethane. They are soft but give the appearance of natural hard rock. *(Stendig Inc., Los Angeles). Courtesy, La Jolla Museum of Contemporary Arts, La Jolla, Calif.*

GIANT CACTUS. Guido Drocco and Franco Mello. 65 inches high, 24 inches deep. Clothes stand made of polyurethane with velour covering. *(Stendig Inc., Los Angeles). Courtesy, La Jolla Museum of Contemporary Art, La Jolla, Calif.*

appendix

ABRASIVE PAPERS

Mesh numbers: Abrasive grains are precision-graded by passing them over a series of screens. Mesh numbers designate the grit sizes. For example, grits that pass through a screen with 80 openings per linear inch are grit 80—designated as 80 (0). (0) is the symbol number.

MESH NO.	SYMBOL	MESH NO.	SYMBOL
Very Fine		*Coarse*	
600	–	80	(0)
500	–	60	(1/2)
411	(10/0)		
360	–	*Very Coarse*	
320	(9/0)	50	(1)
280	(8/0)	40	(1–1/2)
240	(7/0)	36	(2)
		30	(2–1/)
Fine		24	(3)
220	(6/0)	20	(3–1/2)
180	(5/0)	16	(4)
Medium			
150	(3/0)		
120	(0)		
100	(2/0)		

Courtesy, Norton Co., New York

298

Standard measurements for various furniture units offered by the furniture manufacturing industry.

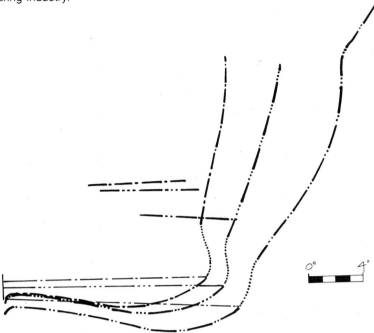

Relative shapes in space of three main types of support for adult seating.

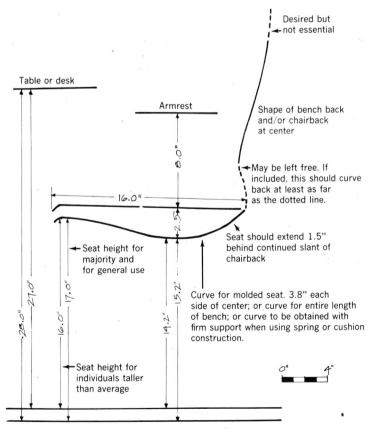

Desired but
not essential

Table or desk

Armrest

Shape of bench back
and/or chairback
at center

May be left free. If
included, this should curve
back at least as far
as the dotted line.

16.0"

6.0"

2.5"

Seat should extend 1.5"
behind continued slant of
chairback

Seat height for
majority and
for general use

Curve for molded seat. 3.8" each
side of center; or curve for entire length
of bench; or curve to be obtained with
firm support when using spring or cushion
construction.

28.0"

27.0"

16.0"

17.0"

15.2"

14.2"

Seat height for
individuals taller
than average

0"   4"

Basic design measurements for chairs and benches used
for dining, writing, or for game tables.

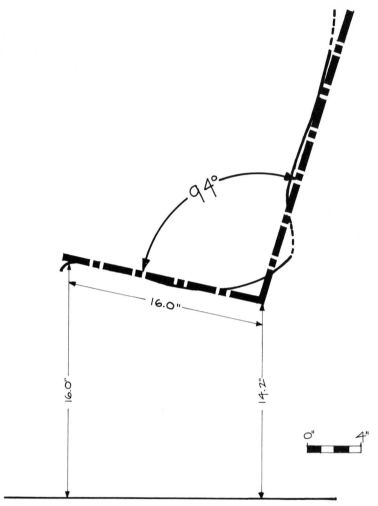

94°

16.0″

16.0″

14.2″

0″   4″

Recommended curved contour for dining for people of average height.

selected bibliography

The number of excellent books available on every period of furniture history is too lengthy to list here. The same is true of books on woodworking techniques, plastics, upholstering, tools, carpentry, and furniture making. A selected bibliography is offered. For additional information consult the library references: *Subject Guide to Books in Print* (for current books) and *The Cumulative Book Index* (for current books and books that are no longer in print but still available through libraries). Check the listings for individual furniture periods and designers. Consult the heading Furniture and related subjects including Design, Finishing, Industry and Trade, Making. Look under wood and related topics, plastics, interior design, and so forth.

Albers, Vernon M., *Advanced Furniture Construction,* A. S. Barnes and Company, London, Thomas Yoseloff, Ltd., 1972.

Andrews, Edward D., and Andrews, Faith, *Religion in Wood: A Book of Shaker Furniture,* Bloomington, Indiana, Indiana University Press, 1966.

Aronson, Joseph, *The Encyclopedia of Furniture,* New York, Crown Publishers, Inc., 1965.

Baker, Hollis S., *Furniture in the Ancient World,* New York, The Macmillan Co., 1965.

Barilli, Renato, *Art Nouveau,* London–New York, Paul Hamlyn, 1966.

Beekman, W. B., *Elsevier's Wood Dictionary,* 3 vols. Amsterdam, London, New York, Elsevier Publishing Company, 1964.

Bishop, Robert, *Centuries and Styles of the American Chair,* 1640–1790, New York, E. P. Dutton & Co., Inc., 1972.

Boericke, Art, and Shapiro, Barry, *Handmade Houses,* San Francisco, Calif., The Scrimshaw Press, 1973.

California Design IX, X, XI, Pasadena, Calif., Pasadena Museum, 1965, 1968, 1971.

Chippendale, Thomas, *The Gentleman and Cabinet Maker's Director,* New York, Dover Publications, Inc., Reprint Edition 1966 of edition published in London, 1752.

De Cristoforo, R. J., *Fun with a Saw,* New York, McGraw-Hill Book Company, Inc., 1962.

———, *Modern Power Tool Woodworking,* Raymond, Mississippi, Magna Publications, 1967.

Delta-Rockwell Craft Library, Pittsburgh, Pa. Series of booklets titled: Getting the Most out of Your: Drill Press; Circular Saw and Joiner; Abrasive Tools; Lathe; Shaper; Band Saw and Scroll Saw; Radial Saw.

Edlin, Herbert L., *What Wood Is That?,* New York, The Viking Press, 1969.

Encyclopaedia Britannica, Chicago, Encyclopaedia Britannica, Inc., 1969. Listings under: Cabinet Furniture; Chair and Sofa; Furniture Design; Wood

Groneman, Chris H., *General Woodworking,* New York, McGraw-Hill Book Company, 1971.

Hammond, James J., Donnelly, Edward T., Harrod, Walter F., and Rayner, Norman A., *Woodworking Technology,* Bloomington, Illinois, McKnight and McKnight Publishing Company, 1972.

Harrar, E. S., Hough's *Encyclopaedia of American Woods,* 13 Vols., New York, Robert Spiller & Sons, 1957.

Hennessey, James, and Papanek, Victor, *Nomadic Furniture,* New York, Pantheon Books, 1973.

Honour, Hugh, *Cabinet Makers and Furniture Designers,* London, George Weidenfeld & Nicolson, Ltd., New York, G. P. Putnam's Sons, 1969.

Hope, Thomas, *Household Furniture and Interior Decoration* (Classic Style Book of the Regency Period), New York, Dover Publications, Inc., 1971.

Kahn, Lloyd, ed., *Shelter,* New York, Random House, 1973.

Katz, Laszlo, *The Art of Woodworking & Furniture Appreciation,* New York, P.F.C. Publishing Co., Inc., 1970.

Knoll International, Inc., *Knoll au Louvre, Catalog of an Exhibition,* New York, Chanticleer Press, Inc., 1972.

Meilach, Dona Z., *Contemporary Art with Wood,* New York, Crown Publishers, Inc., 1968.

———, *Contemporary Leather,* Chicago, Illinois, Henry Regnery Co., 1971.

———, *Papier-Mâché Artistry,* New York, Crown Publishers, Inc., 1971.

———, and Kowal, Dennis, *Sculpture Casting,* New York, Crown Publishers, Inc., 1972.

Mercer, Eric, *Furniture 700–1700,* London, England, George Weidenfeld & Nicolson, Ltd., 1969, U.S., Meredith Press, Des Moines and New York, 1969.

Moody, Ella, *Modern Furniture,* London, Studio Vista Limited; New York, E. P. Dutton & Co., 1966.

———, *New International Encyclopedia of Art,* Vol. 9, New York, The Greystone Press, 1967.

Newman, Thelma R., *Plastics as Sculpture,* Radnor, Pennsylvania, Chilton Book Co., 1974.

Nordness, Lee, *Objects: U.S.A.,* New York, Viking Press, 1970.

Pattou, A. B., *Practical Furniture and Wood Finishing,* Chicago, Frederick J. Drake & Co. Publishers, 1962.

Renwick Gallery, *Woodenworks, Furniture Objects by Five Contemporary Craftsmen.* Exhibition catalog, Minnesota Museum of Art & Smithsonian Institution, 1972.

Robsjohn-Gibbings, T. H., and Pullin, Carlton W., *Furniture of Classical Greece,* New York, Alfred A. Knopf, 1963.

Roukes, Nicholas, *Sculpture in Plastics,* New York, Watson-Guptill, 1968.

Shipway, Verna Cook and Warren, *Mexican Interiors,* New York, Architectural Book Publishing Co., 1962.

Simpson, Thomas, *Fantasy Furniture; Design and Decoration,* New York, Amsterdam, London, Reinhold Book Corporation, 1968.

Sunset Editors, ed., *Furniture You Can Make,* Menlo Park, California, Lane Publishing Co., 1971.

Trussell, John R., *Introducing Furniture Making,* New York, Drake Publishers, Ltd., 1970.

Welding with Wood, *Workrite Products Company,* 1315 South Flower St., Burbank, California.

PUBLICATIONS

Government publications available by writing to the proper department. Charges are subject to change. Some are free.

Department of Agriculture, Washington, D.C. 20250
   The Identification of Furniture Woods Circular No. 66
   Trees, Yearbook 1949

Department of Agriculture, Forest Products
   Laboratory, P.O. Box 5130, Madison, Wisconsin 53705
   Bending Solid Wood to Form No. 25
   Blood Albumin Glues
   Casein Glue
   The Effect of Nail Points on Resistance to Withdrawal
   Important Factors in Gluing with Animal Glue
   Occurrence and Removal of Glue Stains
   Some Methods of Gluing Light Laminated or Plywood Curved Shapes from Veneer
   Strength of Commercial Liquid Glues
   Strong and Weak Glue Joints
   Vegetable Glue
   Wood Handbook

Department of Agriculture, Forest Service, Washington, D.C. 20250
   Hardwoods of the South
   Useful Trees of the United States:
      Birch, No. 22
      Cedar, No. 14
      Eastern Hemlock, No. 10
      Oak, No. 20
      Redwood
      Sweetgum, No. 28
      Western Hemlock, No. 11

Department of Commerce, Superintendent of Documents, Government Printing Office, Washington, D.C. 20402
   American Hardwoods and Their Uses
   American Southern Pine

wood associations

The following professional associations have answered a current questionnaire regarding location and literature available. In some cases, the number of brochures offered was too lengthy to list. Write for titles and price lists. All listings subject to change.

American Plywood Assoc. 1119 A Street Tacoma, Washington 98401	Construction literature catalog of Handy Plans	charges
Appalachian Hardwood Mfg., Inc. Room 408, NCNB Bldg. High Point, North Carolina 27260	Booklets and brochures	free
California Redwood Assoc. 617 Montgomery Street San Francisco, California 94111	Ideas and plans	free or nominal charge
Fine Hardwoods–Amer. Walnut Assoc. 666 Lake Shore Drive Chicago, Illinois 60611	Variety of literature 16mm sound film	charges charges
Hardwood Plywood Mfg. Assoc. P.O. Box 6246 Arlington, Virginia 22206	Technical literature Plans Suppliers	nominal charges
National Hardwood Lumber Assoc. 332 S. Michigan Chicago, Illinois 60604	Technical information	nominal charge
Northern Hardwood & Pine Mfrs. Assn., Inc. 501 Northern Bldg., Green Bay, Wisconsin 54301	Literature, slides	nominal charge

Northeastern Lumber Manufacturers
  Assn., Inc.
13 South Street
Glens Falls, New York 12801
	Literature
	Technical Information
		free
		nominal
		  charge

So. Furniture Mfgrs., Assoc. 209 S. Main St. P.O. Box 951 High Point, North Carolina 27261	Booklets—trade literature	charges
So. Hardwood Lumber Mfg. Assoc. 805 Sterick Bldg. Memphis, Tennessee 38103	Booklets and technical guides	free or nominal charge
Western Wood Products Assoc. 1500 Yeon Bldg. Portland, Oregon 97204	Plans and ideas Product manual	free or nominal charge

index